So, why God?

Twelve sessions for
a children's club

© Steve Hutchinson 2007
First published 2007

ISBN 978 1 84427 222 8

Scripture Union, 207–209 Queensway, Bletchley, Milton Keynes, MK2 2EB, UK
Email: info@scriptureunion.org.uk
Website: www.scriptureunion.org.uk

Scripture Union Australia, Locked Bag 2, Central Coast Business Centre, NSW 2252 Australia
Website: www.scriptureunion.org.au

Scripture Union USA, PO Box 987, Valley Forge, PA 19482, USA
Website: www.scriptureunion.org

Bible quotations have been taken from the Contemporary English Version © American Bible
Society. Anglicisations © British and Foreign Bible Society 1996. Published by
HarperCollinsPublishers and used with permission.

British Library Cataloguing-in-Data
A catalogue for this book is available from the British Library.

Cover design by Kevin Wade, kwgraphicdesign
Cover and internal illustrations by Si Smith

Printed and bound in Great Britain by Henry Ling, Dorchester

So,Why God? is part of eye level, Scripture Union's project to catch up with children and
young people who have not yet caught sight of Jesus.

✍ Scripture Union is an international Christian charity working with churches in more than 130
countries, providing resources to bring the good news of Jesus Christ to children, young people
and families and to encourage them to develop spiritually through the Bible and prayer.
As well as our network of volunteers, staff and associates who run holidays, church-based
events and school Christian groups, we produce a wide range of publications and support
those who use our resources through training programmes.

Thanks to:

Janet Roe and the team who ran the pilot version of
So, Why God? at Lawn Primary School, Swindon

Ro Willoughby, the editor of the original **So, Why God?**
and Alex Taylor who edited this fuller version.

Children everywhere who have asked all these questions
and hundreds more. I hope this book helps some of them
find some of the answers, so that the Lord God
becomes their God too.

eye level clubs...

- are for boys and girls aged 5 to 11.
- are for children who are not yet part of a church (as well as those who are).
- don't assume that children know much about Jesus or have had any experience of church.
- recognise that all children are open to God and the wonder of his world, and that all children can have valid spiritual experiences, regardless of church background.
- aim to give children one of the best hours in the week.
- provide opportunities for appropriate and respectful relationships between children and adults, working in small groups.
- plan to introduce children to the Bible in ways that allow for imagination, exploration and learning difficulties.
- are led by those who long to see children become lifelong followers of Jesus Christ.
- are led by those who will put themselves at a child's level, so that together they can catch sight of Jesus.

Find out about other eye level clubs and contribute to the development of thinking on reaching children who are beyond the church by registering your club at www.scriptureunion.org.uk/streetwise
Your involvment is needed!

Part One: Exploring the Christian faith

Part Two: Hard issues Christians face

Starting out

What is it?

So, Why God? is:

- A course of 12 sessions that enables children to explore the Christian faith using their own questions as a starting point.
- In two halves, the first six sessions helping children to consider God, Jesus and the Bible and how to respond; the second six follow on by looking at hard issues Christians face.
- Based on small-group work with up to eight children and one adult in each group.
- Designed for children between the ages of 7 and 11.
- Made up of hour-long sessions, which can be extended by extra games or craft.

How did it begin?

Many schools have a 'circle time' where children sit around and share something important to them. Some years ago, a Christian teacher asked Steve Hutchinson, the author of **So, Why God?** and a Scripture Union evangelist, to come into a circle time to answer the children's questions about God, Jesus and what it means to be a Christian. Steve has since visited many schools. He is amazed at the range of spiritual questions that children have asked him.

The starting point in **So, Why God?** is not what we want children to learn about the Christian faith but where children already are. All the questions in the course are genuine children's questions. Of course, we hope they will learn about the Christian faith too as they explore their questions.

What are the questions?

PART 1: EXPLORING THE CHRISTIAN FAITH

Why1: What does God look like?
Why2: How did God make people?
Why3: Who was Jesus' real dad, Joseph or God?
Why4: Why did Jesus have to die?
Why5: How did Jesus come back to life?
Why6: How do we know the Bible is true?

PART 2: HARD ISSUES CHRISTIANS FACE

Why7: Do good people go to heaven and bad people go to hell?
Why8: How do you know that you are right about God?
Why9: Why can't you see God?
Why10: How do you know God hears you when you pray?
Why11: Why does God let bad things happen to good people?
Why12: Do you have to go to church to be a Christian?

Whys advice

This is practical guidance, based on the experience of those who have worked with children for years, or advice on issues that leaders need to think about.

We did this

This should give you ideas, as well as the encouragement that someone, somewhere, has done this already! Many of these suggestions come from the pilot run of **So, Why God?** led by Janet Roe at Lawn Junior School, Swindon. Steve is very grateful for the hard work and encouragement involved in running the pilot activity and those that have followed on from it.

When can you use it?

- AFTER A HOLIDAY CLUB
  So, Why God? is especially appropriate to follow up children who are asking questions about the Christian faith. It could be run after school, in the early evening or on a Saturday.
- AS AN AFTER-SCHOOL CLUB
  So, Why God? gives a chance for children to explore their questions in a responsible and caring way. It would be ideal as a follow-up after a visit to *Lifepath*, giving children a further opportunity to look at the faith that was opened up on that day.
- AS PART OF A REGULAR MIDWEEK CLUB
  Some children in a midweek club may be asking serious questions about what it means to follow Jesus. They could be invited to a **So,**

Why God? group as part of the regular club or on a separate occasion.

- AS A LENT COURSE FOR CHILDREN IN THE CHURCH
  If your church or group of churches has an adult Lent course, why not arrange one for children?

We did this

In the pilot group, we met in a school straight after the school day. Eleven children signed up – four boys and seven girls from Year 3 to Year 6. Five of them were in contact with a local church.

Using the two halves of So, Why God?

You would usually start with the first half of **So, Why God?** as it has more basic questions. Then the second half would be used in the following term, to help the children think about questions that come up whilst living as a Christian. There may be occasions when it is better to go straight to the second half, particularly if the children seem to have a good grasp of the Christian faith, and are asking the type of questions covered in the second half.

How to set it up

PEOPLE
Ensure that a group of people are committed to praying for **So, Why God?** Keep pray-ers well informed.

Ensure that you have enough helpers to satisfy the correct child-adult ratio of one adult to every eight children. Extra leaders will be helpful with craft activities.

VENUE
So, Why God? can meet almost anywhere with enough space.

School has the advantage of being neutral ground and familiar territory for children. Carefully explain to the head teacher what it is that you want to do. Be prepared to pay a hire charge for use of school premises. The disadvantage is that local children who do not belong to that particular school are, in effect, excluded if the club meets straight after school.

Church may be more easily available and cheaper. Many of the things you need to run **So, Why God?** may be ready to hand. We want the children to feel at home in church, and this makes follow-up easier.

A community centre or village hall has the advantage of being neutral ground, and often familiar to parents and children. Check that tables and chairs are suitable for children.

Many small groups work well in a home,

though you need to be sure that the home you are using is safe for a group of children, and have structures in place to protect against possible accusations of child abuse.

HEALTH AND SAFETY
Check the premises for health and safety issues. If you are meeting in school this shouldn't be a problem, but make sure you know the fire drill and where the emergency exits are. Get permission to use the nearest phone in an emergency (or bring a mobile phone and check that you have a signal!).

Check the toilets. Are they clearly labelled and clean? If other people have access to them during the **So, Why God?** sessions, do you need to supervise children going to the toilet, to keep them safe?

Make sure you have a first aid kit and know what you should do if a child hurts themselves or becomes ill. Check that you know if any child has allergies or health problems.

Leaders should be covered by a Child Protection Policy and should have CRB clearance (any church or organisation working with children should have a policy already). Make sure all leaders have signed up to it. This helps in looking after children properly and protects leaders. For help with child protection issues, contact the Churches Child Protection Advisory Service (CCPAS) on 0845 120 4550.

We did this

We had run lots of holiday clubs with fun and games in them before, but we wanted **So, Why God?** to be more serious, so we started with a 'Taster' session, for children to decide if they liked it, before agreeing to come to the whole course. In this session we all talked about ourselves and made coats of arms as a craft. (Everyone decided to carry on coming!)

Publicity and permission

Children will only come to **So, Why God?** if they are invited. This can be done with an invitation card, given to all children in a school or church who are likely to be interested. Parents and guardians need to have completed a permission slip by the time of the first session. Instead of invitation cards, you could write a letter to parents inviting their children to come, and have a permission form as a tear-off slip at the bottom.

The letter or invitation card should make clear: what exactly it is that children are coming to; what time it will start and end; the dates of each session; where it is happening; who the leaders are and a phone number for enquiries. If you have done holiday clubs or other special events for children, it is important to explain how this is different.

The permission form for parents or carers to sign should include:

• name of child
• address
• phone number in case of emergency
• date of birth (or age)
• who will be collecting them, if not a parent or carer
• special needs (such as food allergies, if you are offering refreshments)
• a space for parent's or carer's signature

Groups

If you have fewer than eight children, stay together as one group throughout. With more than eight, divide into smaller groups, with an adult in each one. Keep the same groups throughout the course.

Why in

The children should go straight into groups as they arrive, where there should be something for them to do. These activities are designed to start as soon as the first child arrives, with others joining in. Provide suitable refreshments, taking into account any allergy issues.

So, Why God?

Sit round in a circle, either on the floor or around a table, to involve everyone. This time includes various activities, some presented by a leader, others worked out together.

Why me?

Move back to groups for either a craft activity or to complete a little booklet: **My Why Book!** for Why1–6 and **What do you think?** for Why7–12. These booklets help to explore the questions further. You cannot do both activities if your whole session is an hour. On a school day, many children will have had enough of writing and working on puzzles, so a craft activity will probably suit them better. Others enjoy working at little books, so will want **My Why Book!** and **What do you think?** You can photocopy pages 45–50 and pages 77–80 to produce these booklets. (Photocopy double sided, cut horizontally along the continuous line then fold each page along the dotted line. Gather the pages together in page number order, and staple in the centre to make a book.)

Craft

Some preparation beforehand is usually needed. Often a sample 'Here's one I made earlier' helps children. This is an opportunity to talk and build relationships, not just to make a perfect craft item!

Praying together

At the end of the group time, pray together, encouraging participation.

Postbox

Many children like to write notes to their leaders. The Postbox gives a chance for this, along with the opportunity to ask questions and send in jokes and pictures.

So, Who is God? link

At the end of some sessions there is a link to relevant questions in *So, Who is God?* (SU) Robert Willoughby, ISBN 1 84427 123 4

What does each session look like?

The suggested programme lasts an hour. Adapt it to suit your group.

WHY IN (In small groups)	Various way-in activities	10 minutes
SO, WHY GOD? (All together) **What do you know?** or **On the spot** **What does the Bible say?** **What's the story?** **What's the answer?**	Quiz or interview Introducing the Bible Retold Bible story This session's question	5 minutes 5 minutes 10 minutes 5 minutes
WHY ME? (In small groups) **What can I do?** **What now?**	Craft activity or **My Why Book!** Prayer and final round-up	20 minutes 5 minutes

What sort of leaders does So, Why God? need?

- People who really care for children, and want them to come to know God.
- People who accept that they don't know all the answers, but are prepared to find out and help others to do the same.
- People who know God for themselves and are willing to think hard about how to share what they know of God with children.
- People who are willing to let the children's own questions determine the way the session runs, even if it means not getting through the prepared material.

So, why do children ask these questions?

Children have a natural spirituality. They want to know about God, whoever he is. Many children with no religious background at all believe that there must be a God somewhere out there. We shouldn't be surprised when children's questions about God move on to talking about ghosts or other supernatural phenomena.

However, spirituality is not just about believing in God. In school, teachers encourage children to respond to nature with awe. This is the 'Wow!' factor. It comes naturally to children. Our responsibility is to tap into this natural interest in something outside our normal, visible world, and introduce the children to God.

Whys advice

Issues which concern adults are not necessarily the ones that bother children. Leaders need to be sensitive to the questions children are actually asking, and to have thought out their own answers from the Bible. They then need to work out how to explain them to the children!

What is a child's world like?

It's essential to find out as much as you can about the world of a child. Church children will have different questions from those of other faiths or from a no faith background. Think carefully how each session will relate to a child. Watch children's TV, and talk with them about what they watch and read.

We live in a multi-faith society. Children learn about the beliefs and practices of other faiths in RE at school. This can lead to some confusion in identifying which faith believes what. In some sessions children's awareness of other faiths will become obvious. In Why6, for example, you may discover they have heard about the sacred texts of other faiths, as well as the Bible, but they may not have understood what the difference is between the Qur'an, the Bible and the Hindu Scriptures.

We can speak with confidence about what Christians believe and the truth that the only way to come to God is through Jesus Christ. However, at all times, we need to be respectful towards other faith positions. If you have a child from another faith background, be particularly sensitive and avoid making sweeping judgements.

Church children

Don't assume that children who attend church will know much about God. They may be quicker to volunteer answers than others, but many can have mixed-up ideas. They may be familiar with the vocabulary and concepts of the Christian faith without actually understanding them.

Children with special needs

We want to make our activities open to all. Every child has different needs, but some are specifically described in education as having 'special needs', which can include physical difficulties/illnesses, learning difficulties or behavioural or emotional problems. It is wise to ask parents or teachers for advice in order to provide adequate help or resources. Often it is enough for a child to be accepted and loved, but sometimes it will mean a leader coming specifically to help one child. Let the child join in as much as possible.

Whys advice

For more information about working with children with special needs, check out *Top Tips on Welcoming Special Children* (SU, £2.99, 1 84427 126 9). It is a book full of biblically based, practical ideas!

Using the Bible with children

So, Why God? starts with children's questions, and looks at what the Bible has to say in response. The retold Bible story helps children see how God has related to his people over the years. We also want the children to engage with the Bible itself, so that they too can hear from God directly. We don't want merely to tell them what is in the Bible. The questions we ask should be guided, but open-ended. There is not always one right answer! It is vital to be imaginative so that all children, whatever their reading ability, can access the Bible. Suggestions have been given in each session.

The *Contemporary English Version* has been used in **So, Why God?** The *Good News Bible* is also suitable for children. If you are keen on the NIV, try using the NIrV (r for readers). It is based on the NIV but much simpler, and so easier for children.

Helping children respond
Prayer card
When helping a child to make a decision to become a follower of Jesus, why not use a simple booklet or prayer card? This will focus the discussion and give the child something to take away with them. A sample prayer card is printed on page 17. Photocopy this onto card. Three suitable booklets to help are *Friends with Jesus* (5 to 7s); *Me + Jesus* (8 to 9s); *Jesus=friendship forever* (10 to 12s) all from Scripture Union. (See page 76 for more details.)

The prime aim of **So, Why God?** is to enable children to respond to the story of God's love for us. As a leader it will be helpful if you:

- Let the child do most of the talking and questioning. Listen carefully to be sure you are answering the question being asked.
- Keep the conversation short and simple. Children can't concentrate for too long.
- Don't put pressure on children to respond. **So, Why God?** is about helping every child to know enough about the Christian faith to be able to make up their own mind. One way to avoid undue pressure is to give the child a choice: 'Would you like to pray with me now, or pray on your own when you are ready?'

How to finish each half of So, Why God?
So, Why God? is in two halves deliberately. Each half has different aims and different types of questions. Doing one half each term fits better for most groups, and may make it easier for children to come for the whole course. It is important to finish each half of the **So, Why God?** course on a positive note. So do something special after Why6 and Why12. Here are some suggestions.

A party
Organise a celebratory party, something for the children to remember. This could be during Why6 or as an extra session given over to a fun and games party, with a brief time to review what they have learnt.

Snapshots through Mark is a booklet which contains twenty-four days of Bible reading material through Mark and Acts. It looks at what it means to have Jesus as King in our lives and to follow him. The group time for Why6 introduces children to *Snapshots through Mark*. To encourage the children to continue using it, you could ask them to bring their copy to church or the school Christian group to show you, and could even offer a small prize to everyone who completes it. The prize might include the next dated issue of *Snapshots*, SU's Bible reading material for 8 to 11s.

Parents' evening
Extend Why6 and Why12 and invite parents and carers to join you. Certificates could be awarded and craft shown. Take the opportunity to explain what you have been doing. Some parents will be amazed at the questions their children have asked. There may be interest in an adult course such as the Alpha Course. Refreshments help such an event to go well.

Film show or presentation to the whole school or church
A presentation at the end, whether to parents, the school or the church, helps to review what has been discovered and gives **So, Why God?** added importance to the children.

We did this
We had a celebration party. At the end, children talked about what they could do next. They were offered Bible reading notes and a Bible to borrow if they didn't have a suitable one at home. The pilot project showed the film *The Miracle Maker* to the whole school.

Photocopy this planning page, and then fill it in with the other leaders when you plan each session. Fill in the evaluation and attendance sections afterwards to have a complete record of what you have done.

So, Why God? Session Plan

Session: Date: Team:

Overall aim:

Resources needed:

Brief session plan (with initials for the team member leading)
1
2
3
4
5
6
7

Attendance: (List the names of all those who came to the session.)

Evaluation: (How well do you think the session went? Be positive, eg what worked well?)

CLUE ONE

This is Mary. Draw what has made her so shocked.

CLUE TWO

What did the angel tell Joseph?

RRAMY RAMY! TEH BBAY'S NMEA SI EJSSU

CLUE THREE

Can you remember the memory verse?

CLUE FOUR

Everyone can do this.

Find Luke 2:1–4 and answer these questions.

Who was the Emperor?

Where did everyone have to go?

Where did Joseph leave?

Who had lived in Bethlehem?

CLUE FIVE

Spot eight differences in the pictures below.

CLUE SIX

In 15 seconds, think of as many words as you can to describe what the shepherds felt when the angels appeared.

CLUE SEVEN

Everyone quickly draw a picture of what the shepherds found when they came to worship Jesus.

(Check how correct their pictures are by looking at Luke 2:15–20.)

CLUE EIGHT

Read out loud Luke 2:19.
*   What did Mary keep on doing?
*   Why did she keep doing these things?

CLUE NINE

Find Matthew 2:7–12 and answer these questions:
*   What did King Herod ask the wise men?
*   Did he really want to worship this king?
*   What led the wise men to Jesus?
*   Where was Jesus?
*   What gifts did they give to him?
*   What stopped them going back to King Herod?

CLUE TEN
Which of these two are the same?

Use with Why4

Prayer card

How can I ask Jesus to be my friend?

God sent Jesus to show us how much he loves us. He wants us to love and trust him. He wants each one of us to be his friends. We need to be sorry for the wrong things that we have done – really sorry so we don't want to do them again. We need to believe that Jesus died on the cross so that we could be forgiven. If you want to be a friend of Jesus, you can pray like this:

Jesus, I want to be your friend.
Thank you that you love me.
Thank you for living in the world and dying on a cross for me.
I'm sorry for all the wrong things I have done.
Please forgive me and let me be your friend.
Please may the Holy Spirit help me be like you.
Amen.

God hears us when we pray to him and has promised to forgive us and help us to be his friends if we really want to.
This card belongs to:

Name ....

Date...

If you have prayed this prayer and you are really serious about being friends with Jesus, we would like to know so we can help you. Please fill in this part of the card, tear it off and give it back to the person who gave you the prayer card. Or if you go to a club with a Postbox, put it in there.

Name..

Address...

....

....

Postcode..

Use with Why 2

Name....................................

What is your favourite bird or animal or plant? Why?

_____

_____

What do you think is the most beautiful place in the world? Why?

_____

_____

What's your favourite sound in nature? Why?

_____

_____

What's your favourite colour? Why?

_____

_____

Use with Why11

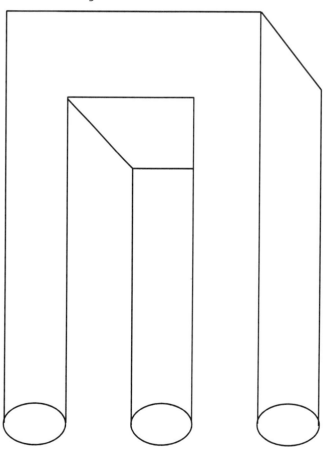

Use with Why6

Use with Why 7

You are invited to THE BEST PARTY EVER!

Why1

Exodus 3:1–15

Aim **To look at what God is like and to encourage children to ask questions and find answers about the character of God.**

What does God look like?

What's it all about?

Children more often ask what God looks like, as opposed to what God is like. This is because they are used to assessing people's character by what they look like. If you ask them about their new teacher, they will often tell you that she looks really nice, or that the head teacher at their new school looks really cross all the time! So, when children ask what God looks like, it is fair to assume they are also interested in what his character is like. This session will cover the facts that:

- God exists.The Bible assumes this and so does not give us many answers to the question, 'Does God exist?'
- God is loving and caring
- God communicates with people
- We can have a personal relationship with him.

What sort of leaders does Why1 need?

It is important to remember that leaders don't have to know all the answers. Listen to the children, and let them ask their own questions. In Why1, a leader has the opportunity to explain the answer to the question, 'What does God look like?' Further discussion may show that the children don't really understand what has been said. Don't be tempted to go over the same explanation yet again – try a different approach.

These notes give a number of explanations to answer the question, but work out your own answers. Why1 needs leaders who have taken time to think and pray about ways to help children understand more about God.

So, why does this question matter?

Many people today are completely secular with no understanding of or commitment to any god or religion. We live in a multi-faith society, a society where we pick 'n' mix what we do or don't believe. Many people who are seeking spirituality create a god to their own liking.

Before we can encourage children to believe in God, we must consider what God is like.

- What sort of a God do we believe in?
- What has he done?
- What is he like?
- What does he want us to do?

So, why do children ask, 'What does God look like?'

Children have a natural spirituality. They want to know what is beyond what they can see or touch. They want to know about God, whoever he is. They may not mean the God whose activity fills the pages of the Bible. They may have no religious background at all, but believe that there must be a god out there somewhere.

Children pick up all sorts of ideas about God. In school assemblies there is often a mention of God. Children may be encouraged to pray to him or think about him, but they may have some really muddled ideas. **So, Why God?** could become a forum for picking up on a whole range of ways that God comes into children's lives.

Many church children will have grown up with a basic Christian understanding of God and his Son, Jesus, but may be confused by their non-Christian friends.

Whys advice

Listen to children (inside and outside the church community) talking about things that excite them or cause them to wonder. How do they express it? Listen to how they use the name of God in conversation.

The programme for each session is tight. Leaders need to be well prepared to fit everything in, but it is always better for the children to be fully occupied, rather than allowing them to get bored or distracted! Keep the session moving and make sure you are ready to move on quickly to the next item.

Why in

◐1 A picture of God
(10 minutes)

Give out refreshments as the children arrive, if appropriate. Find out what they have done in the day. Arrange the children in groups beforehand, if possible putting friends together and separating those who argue. Children usually like to be with others of the same age.

Give the children a piece of paper, pencils and crayons. Ask them to draw what they think God looks like. If you want their real thoughts, don't give them any ideas at all. As they draw, chat with them about what they are drawing and why. If you have someone who does not believe in God at all, ask if they believe in any other gods or very special people – they could draw their favourite famous person. (Don't give this option to the whole group, or they may miss out on drawing their idea of God.)

Be ready with suggestions, if necessary, to get children started. Some children may think God is an old man with a beard, wearing a sheet. Maybe they imagine someone holding the whole world in his hands. Others will draw him like an old uncle who is always giving out sweets, or maybe like an angry, strict person, trying to catch us being naughty. Some might draw a picture of Jesus. Look at the pictures the children have drawn, and discuss the similarities and differences. Most children will draw God in some sort of human form. Why have they drawn God as a person? Can we talk with something that is not a person? Sow that seed in their minds. Ask the children if you can keep their pictures, making sure they have put their names on them. These pictures will help you, as a leader, get to know the children. You could use them later in the session, or in a future **So, Why God?**

We did this
One girl drew a man with two enormous ears, 'because God always listens!' Some older girls left their paper blank, as 'God is invisible!'

So, Why God?

◐1 What do you know?
(5 minutes)

Every child should be able to participate. A quiz can also help you to identify the knowledge of each child present. Begin with some general knowledge questions, so as not to disadvantage anyone, and then move on to some Bible questions, if you think they are appropriate. Divide the children into two teams.

You can make up your own, but here are some questions to get you started:

1   What is the capital city of Italy? (Rome)
2   Who wrote 'The Lion, the Witch and the Wardrobe'? (C S Lewis)
3   What is the name of the Tweenies' dog? (Doodles or Izzles)
4   What does the 'www' in an internet address stand for? (World Wide Web)
5   Which river runs through London? (The Thames)
6   In what year did a human being first walk on the moon? (1969)
7   What is the second film in the original *Star Wars* trilogy called? (*The Empire Strikes Back*)
8   Which bird can fly backwards? (Hummingbird)
9   What number do you get if you add the number of days in a week to the number of months in a year, and then subtract the number of players in a football team? (7 + 12 - 11 = 8)
10 What colour do you get if you mix blue and yellow together? (Green)

Whys advice
It can be great fun to use unusual ways of keeping the score in a quiz. For example, give some Lego bricks to each team. Each time a child gives a correct answer, they throw a dice and take the corresponding number of Lego bricks to add to a brick tower. The highest tower at the end wins.

◑2 What does the Bible say?
(5 minutes)

INTRODUCTION TO THE BIBLE
Explain that we have the Bible to help us answer our questions about God, his world and how he wants us to live. It is not always an easy book to read, but it contains all the things that God wants us to know, so it is worth making the effort. Explain simply how the Bible works; for example that it has two parts, the Old and New Testaments.

You could go on to talk about books, chapters and verses and then explain the different types of writing that are used in the Bible. Most children know a little about different styles of writing such as poems, letters or stories. The Bible has all of these, and more. Use your own

1

Bible to show each of these features as you talk about them.

Each time you come to **So, Why God?** you will be reading a bit of the Bible. This time we will look at a story from the Old Testament.

⏱3 What's the story?
(10 minutes)

Bible story: Exodus 3:1–15
Moses and the burning bush

Use the illustrations on page 12 as you tell the story. You could enlarge them on a photocopier, then colour them in. Or you could put them on acetates.

God appeared to Moses (v 2). It is one of the few times in the Bible that God showed himself in a physical form so that people could see him.

BEGINNING
God's people, the Israelites, were in big trouble. They lived in Egypt, but they were foreigners, and the Egyptians didn't like them. Explain just how hard it was.
(Illustration 1)
A man called Moses had a very unusual upbringing. His mum and dad were Israelites, but Moses had been brought up in the royal palace so he looked and sounded like an Egyptian. Then, one day, he saw an Egyptian kill an Israelite man. Moses was furious. How dare anyone kill one of his own people?! In his fury he killed the Egyptian, but he was so scared that he would be punished that he ran away.
(Illustration 2)
He married, and became a shepherd, looking after hundreds of sheep, in an area where there wasn't much grass or water.

MIDDLE
Introduce the Bible at this point. You could put the words on an acetate, help the children find Exodus 3:1–6, or invite the children to listen as you read it yourself, using as much expression as possible.
(Illustration 3)
At the point where Moses sees the bush on fire, you could light a candle, taking all necessary safety precautions.
(Illustration 4)
Then in your own words explain what Moses saw and the conversation that he had with God. Keep it simple but clear. Tell the children how amazing it was that God was speaking to a person. Moses was scared stiff, so he covered his face. Explain about God's wonderful plan, and what he wanted Moses to do. This was all because God cared for his people. (Include some

of the questions that Moses asked God, since **So, Why God?** is all about asking questions.)

ENDING
Explain how God wants to talk with and listen to us, just as he did all those years ago. He cares for us just as he cared for his people in Egypt. He wants us to get to know him.

Whys advice
Telling a story needs:
A BEGINNING – find an attention-grabbing way to lead into the story.
A MIDDLE – be sure you know why you are telling the story. One main point is enough for children.
AN ENDING – know how you will finish. Don't just read the story from the Bible, but tell it in your own words. Some children will have seen the film *Prince of Egypt* (which follows the Bible fairly closely) so will be familiar with the story.

⏱4 What's the answer?
(5 minutes)

This is an impossible question to answer because God's appearance is not described in the Bible. He does not have a recognisable shape and so we don't know the answer to this question. But we can get an idea of what God is like by what he has said and done.

To introduce this idea, play this telephone conversation game. Record several voices of people whom the children don't know. Make sure there is a mixture of soft and rough, slow and quick, strong accents, male, female. Let each voice give a few clues about the person: where they work, their identity, interests, family relationships etc. The aim is not for the children to guess who it is but to work out what they can know about this person. Begin by playing one of the voices.

For example: 'Hello! (Sounding a bit out of breath.) I nearly didn't answer the phone because I have just come in from work. My brand new car broke down on the way home. But fortunately my son, who is a car mechanic, was in. I rang him on my mobile and he drove out straightaway. "It'll only take a minute, Dad/Mum!" he said, and he fixed it. So I've just got in.'

What can the children tell you about this person even though they can't see them? Get them to think about the gender, age, relationships, daily routine and quality of their voice. Continue by playing each of the voices in turn.

Explain that in the same way we have lots of

clues to tell us what God's character is like. First of all, talk about the fact that he has created the world. What sort of person does that make him? Let the children use their imaginations as they talk. If you can, get hold of the poem *My dad* by Steve Turner, (from *The day I fell down the toilet* (Lion)) and read it after your discussion. It is worth reading more than once. Let the children wonder at the greatness of God.

Whys advice

When you are all together, it is simplest just to sit in a circle on the floor, most comfortably on a piece of carpet. This encourages involvement and discussion. One way of keeping talkative children in order is to pass a teddy bear or something similar around. Only the person holding the teddy can speak. Adults need to join in with the circle on the same level as the children. If you are a small group, sitting round a table will work well. Make sure everyone in the circle can see and hear everyone else.

Why me?

⏱1 What can I do?
(20 minutes)

As you work in your groups, talk about the pictures that the children drew at the start, and what the children now think about what God looks like. Choose either *My Why Book!* or Craft activity.

My Why Book!

Each child will need their own copy and a pen, pencil and crayons. The aim is not merely to fill in the right answers, but to help children learn how to find their own answers, particularly from the Bible.

Craft: A Collage

The story of Moses and the burning bush lends itself to a large collage picture for the group to work on together. This is a good first activity, as the children share in the project.
Draw a large outline of the picture of the

burning bush from the previous page, onto a large sheet of card. You will need to enlarge it. (Do it roughly by eye with pencil, then make a strong outline with a felt-tip pen, or ask someone who likes to draw if you don't feel confident!) Collect material scraps, magazines, sand, pasta, silver paper, crêpe paper and anything else that can be stuck on. Think about the colours that the picture will need. Use white PVA glue to stick the objects onto the picture.

⏱2 What now?
(5 minutes)

Talk with God together. Prayers could include thanking God that we can talk with him and know him, thanking him for the world he has made, and asking him to help us answer the children's specific questions. Invite the children to speak with God. Next time they may feel more comfortable in doing this, but explain that prayer is simply speaking out loud to God.

Postbox

At the end of the session, encourage the children to write down any questions they may want to ask, and put them into the box. Children could also write jokes, draw pictures or write letters to the leaders. If there is no time at the end, children could write their messages at home to put in the Postbox next time. All this helps to encourage children to ask questions that may be answered. Their contributions matter!

Whys advice

Children sometimes find it easier to pray out loud if they write down their prayer first. If you want to stick their prayers up somewhere, they could write them on Post-it notes. These could be stuck on to a picture of a tree or a rainbow.

So, Who is God? **link**
This question is also answered in *So, Who is God?*, Question 11 (page 44) if the children would like to read another viewpoint. Question 1 is also helpful and refers to the same Bible story.

Why2

**Genesis 1:26–28;
Genesis 2:4b–24**

Aims **To show that God
created this amazing
world.
To think about why we
were made and what it
means to be made in God's
image. What does that
make me?**

How did God make people?

What's it all about?
- God made humans to be like himself
- God blessed humans and gave them a fantastic place to live
- He gave them control over the animals, birds and all living creatures and commanded them to care for the world
- God created us to have relationships with other people
- He also made us to have a relationship with him. He was, and is, committed to us and our world.

What sort of leaders does Why2 need?
Children learn far more by observing what we do and how we act than from listening to what we say. Children will look to us to discover what God is like. When we talk about having a relationship with him, they will want to hear about our own experiences.

God's world is fantastically made (even though we also know it is deeply damaged). Leaders need to be people who marvel at the wonders of creation and can identify with children's enthusiasms.

So, why does this question matter?
Many Christian adults are divided over what they believe about creation and evolution. Some believe that God literally created the world in six 24-hour periods; others believe that the days should not be interpreted literally; some believe that God created by means of evolution. It's important to be aware that not everyone may agree with you, including some of the other leaders. Try to avoid being dogmatic.

The Bible teaches that man and woman were created in the image of God, and set apart from the animal kingdom. Almost all children long to have relationships, either to be in a gang or to have close friends. Many will have been damaged by broken relationships within their families. They may find it very difficult to make relationships. Some children will be naturally shy.

Others will be very demanding of a relationship. We have been made by God to be in relationships with others. Children will know this from experience, but may not realise that it is God who thought of friendships in the first place.

An increasing number of children suffer from poor self-image. They lack confidence, feel worthless and even hate themselves. Be particularly sensitive to this possibility as you get to know each child. It is great news that God has made you to be like him and to be his friend, and that he has a role for each for us. Look for ways to share this with the children.

We did this
We made a special effort to be ready for early arrivals. We had time to chat with them, catching up on their news and building friendships. It was hard work to make sure we were ready on time, but it was worth it!

So, why do children ask, 'How did God make people?'
Children love making things, and finding out how things are made. As they grow older, they ask about their own origins, thinking about where they came from and why they were made. They are fascinated by planets, and ask, 'How did they get there?' or, 'What's a supernova?'

Many children are great animal lovers, often treating a pet as a close friend. Some children feel passionately about animal abuse. Are animals the same as humans? Genesis makes it clear that God has a relationship with human beings that he doesn't have with other creatures. Children often have questions about evolution, but it is important not to get bogged down with this or that theory. Say that Christians believe that the world did not come about by accident, but was made by God, however he went about it! If a child asks if you believe in evolution, answer honestly but emphasise that this is something about which people hold lots of different opinions.

Church children

Children who have grown up knowing the Biblical creation story may have encountered conflicts between what they learn at church, or from their parents, and what they hear at school. As they grow older, they will try to sort out what they themselves believe, rather than simply accepting their parents' beliefs. This session of **So, Why God?** provides an opportunity to discuss such beliefs in small groups which can be very helpful to them.

Why in

1 Making things
(10 minutes)

In the same small groups as last time, ask the children to make something using basic materials. It doesn't really matter what you make, or what materials you use, but it needs to be simple. For example, choose one of the following:

- A big box of Lego, or some other construction set, gives children the chance to make something fairly quickly.
- If you can do any origami, teach the children to make a simple paper model. Practise beforehand, preferably by showing a child how to make it. Then you will discover what they find difficult.
- Modelling balloons are very popular (but you need to know how to use them). A starter kit and practice is the best way to find out. These can be bought at a craft shop or a balloon specialist shop.
- Provide boxes, card, paper, scraps of material with PVA glue and ask the children to construct a junk building. You won't have time for any paint. It takes too long to dry and is messy!

Whys advice

This sort of activity gets you off to a good start; the purpose is:

- to make allowances for children who arrive at different times
- to help them wind down after school
- to involve them right from the start
- to get to know each other
- to introduce the question for this session.

So, Why God?

1 On the spot
(5 minutes)

Later in the course, you could have an 'On the spot' time, when a leader will answer questions from the Postbox, but the second session is probably too early to do this. Prepare the children for future times, when they will have the chance to quiz a leader. Today, everyone is 'On the spot'. Give everyone the questionnaire at the bottom of page 17.

2 What does the Bible say?
(5 minutes)

God's creation

If we want to know the answer to this question, we should look in the Bible. The Bible isn't a how-to manual, though, and we learn more about 'why' than 'how'. Ask if anyone can remember something about the Bible from the last So, Why God? session.

Ask one child to read out Genesis 2:4b–7 or encourage all the children to read it, then give each child some clay or play dough and ask them to make the shape of a person. As they do this, read out Genesis 1:1 – 2:4. You may wish to select just a few verses to read.

Whys advice

To make play dough for eight people
Mix together 2 teaspoons cream of tartar, 1 cup flour, 1/2 cup salt, 1 tablespoon oil, 1 cup water and food colouring. Heat slowly stirring all the time until the dough comes away from the side of the pan. Knead the warm dough for 3 to 4 minutes. Once cool, store in an airtight container/plastic bag.

3 What's the story?
(10 minutes)

Bible story: Genesis 2:15–23

GOD MADE THE WORLD

A natural way to lead on from the questionnaire is to read and tell part of the story from Genesis. This emphasises the fact that God cared so much that he gave the first man everything he needed, including a companion. Use the artwork on page 13 to tell the story. Enlarge the illustrations using a photocopier, then either stick them on a board

2

or wall with double-sided tape or Blu-tack, or use Velcro to stick onto a board covered in loop nylon. Alternatively, photocopy the illustrations onto acetate and use an overhead projector.

Whys advice

A Velcro board can be made by sticking loop nylon material on to plywood. Velcro will then fix items to the board. For further help contact Steve Hutchinson via Scripture Union (steveh@scriptureunion.org.uk).

BEGINNING

We might think that God had a problem. He'd created a man, who was known as Adam, and put him in the Garden of Eden to look after it. The garden was a wonderful place with lots of beautiful plants and flowers to look at and smell, and the trees were full of fruit *(Illustration 1)*. So what was the problem? The man was lonely.

MIDDLE

God knew that Adam needed a friend. It wasn't good for him to be alone. God had made some animals, and they can be good friends. Adam gave names to all the animals – how many can you think of in one minute? But not one of them was suitable to be a real friend *(Illustration 2)*. So God put the man to sleep and took out one of his ribs. God made a woman from that rib, and brought her to the man. The man said something like, 'Oh, wow! At last! That's great!' *(Illustration 3)*.

ENDING

God knows all about us. His love for humans has never stopped. He knows we need friends. In fact, he wants us to be good friends with him as well. He even wants boys and girls to be good friends with each other! (But remembering what junior children are like, perhaps that will have to wait a few years!)

At last, here was someone who could be a real friend; someone to talk with and someone who would help him look after the animals *(Illustration 4)*.

⊕4 What's the answer?
(5 minutes)

Ask the children these questions as a discussion starter.

- What is it about your models that stops them moving?
- Can you begin to imagine how God gave life? What are some of the things about us that show that we are alive? (We can move, talk, smell, see, etc.)

The most important part of the answer to the question lies in the fact that we are modelled on God himself. That is how God wanted us to be made. It didn't happen just by chance. God made us to be like himself – that's why we are different from animals. Children will naturally think that this means we look like God, but since we don't know what God looks like, it means more about what we are like inside as people. This would be a good opportunity to remind them of what they thought about last time.

Harder questions

- What can make us think that we are an accident, or we don't matter? (You could make up an imaginary story about a child whom nobody ever listened to and who ended up thinking that no one cared.) Be very sensitive as you talk about this, as some of the children (or adults) may feel this already.
- What difference does it make that God made humans to be special? God made us and planned for us to be alive. What does God think when you feel bad about yourself? (Some children feel bad about themselves when they have done wrong, which is not necessarily a bad thing!)

It is quite likely that the discussion will include these questions, so be prepared for them. If the children don't ask them, you may want to introduce them anyway if there is time.

- What about the dinosaurs?
- What about evolution that we learn in schools?

Be prepared to say that you don't know the answer to a question, but that you will try to discover the answer for the next time you meet.

2

Whys advice
Further reading for leaders:
Reason, Science and Faith, Roger Forster and Paul Marsden, (Wits and Stock) has very detailed arguments about creation and evolution.
The Facts of Life, Richard Milton (Corgi) has lots of good information about recent research into evolution and the problems with accepting it (not written from a Christian perspective).
Also worth reading, *God and Science,* Wilkinson & Frost (Monarch).

Why me?

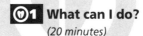 **What can I do?**
(20 minutes)

As you talk together, remember the pictures the children drew or things they made at the start and lead the discussion on from there. Use either **My Why Book!** or the craft option here.

Craft: a creation scene in a shoebox

Be sure to have made one of these earlier, to inspire the children. Check which parts are more difficult, or may take the children a long time. You may need to do some cutting out in advance, particularly if you feel the children will struggle with this.

You will need:
- a shoebox for each child (shoe shops will often save you some if you ask them far enough in advance)
- pictures of Adam, Eve, some animals and plants for the garden, copied onto thin card (you could adapt the ones from page 13
- paper for the background
- glue sticks and child-safe scissors
- pencils, crayons and felt-tip pens

Put the shoebox on the background paper and draw round it. Cut out just inside the outline to leave a piece of paper that will fit neatly inside the bottom of the shoebox to become the background. Before gluing it in, decorate the scene with the sky, sun, and some trees and bushes, and then glue it to the inside bottom of the box. Cut three slits in the base of the box.

Colour in pictures of Adam, Eve, a tree or an animal. Cut them out, leaving a tab at the bottom. Fold down the tab, and use it to stick the figures and animals inside the slits in the base. Don't forget to put names on the shoeboxes.

⊙2 What now?
(5 minutes)

At the end of the group time, talk with God together. Prayers could include thanking God that we can talk with him and know him, and for the world he has made; and asking him to help us answer specific questions.

Ask the children to write down or draw one thing that God has made. Then go round in a circle and each person say 'Thank you God for _____.'

Postbox
Remind the children about writing letters, questions, jokes or ideas to put in the Postbox. If there is time before the children leave, help them to write a letter.

***So, Who is God?* link**
So, Who is God? has Question 2 (page 12) which is very similar, and Question 18 (page 72) also relates to the topic.

Why3

Matthew 1:18–25;
Luke 2:1–20

Aims **To focus on the Christmas story, probably the Bible story children know best.
To help children think about where Jesus came from.
To cause children to wonder that God could become a human being and so understand what it is like to be human.**

Who was Jesus' real dad, Joseph or God?

What's it all about?

Introducing Jesus

The children may have found it hard to picture God in the last two sessions. That's partly why Jesus came – as a human being – so that we can see what God is like.

The most well-known Bible story

The Christmas story is probably the most well known of the stories in the Bible, which is a key reason for including it in **So, Why God?** It builds upon what children are already familiar with.

What sort of leaders does Why3 need?

Since this session introduces Jesus to our discussions, it is important for leaders to review their own relationship with him. It is vital that we are meeting with him regularly, as we read the Bible and pray.

Adults are so familiar with the Christmas story that it may have lost its appeal, so leaders need to be prepared to rediscover the story for themselves. As a start, read the Bible verses given at the start of this section carefully. Look for the real Christmas story, not the traditional one. Try *Behind the Scenes Christmas* (SU, 978 1 84427 190 0).

So, why does this question matter?

The nature of Jesus is fundamental to the Christian faith. Jesus is both fully God and fully human. Many early heresies came about as people grappled to understand this. Modern cults usually depart from an orthodox Christian position over what they believe about Jesus. The apparently simple question of Jesus' fatherhood becomes a key question about Jesus: Who is he really? Where did he come from? What should we believe about him?

So, why do children ask, 'Who was Jesus' real dad, Joseph or God?'

They think they have caught us out

At Christmas children hear that Jesus' mum and dad are Mary and Joseph. By Easter we are telling them that Jesus is the Son of God. The clever ones think about this and say both can't be right!

Diverse family structures

Children grow up in different types of families. They may live with only one parent. Some children may not know who their father is. There are step-parents or foster parents, half-brothers or stepsisters, adopted children, children with no parents and those living with both. Some will know that they look or behave like a parent; others won't. Children are interested in, and sometimes uncertain about, their roots.

Harry Potter (and others)

One of the striking features of the Harry Potter stories is that Harry's origins and his parents' identity are crucial to his understanding of who he is. Other people's memories of his (dead) parents fundamentally affect the way people relate to him, and the expectations they have of him. It matters where you come from.

The mishmash of Christmas

For children, Christmas is a wonderful mixture of Santa, shepherds, stars, presents, parties, stables, fun and wise men, all rolled into one. Be aware of this as you talk with the children. They may be shocked at how the Bible tells the story. Father Christmas didn't make an appearance in the stable! Is the Christian faith simply a collection of 'fairy' stories which may turn out to be untrue?

Church children

Most church children will know a lot about Jesus. They will know the 'right answers' about him. They may be able to parrot the words 'Jesus is the Son of God', but not have thought about what this means. The Christmas story is a brilliant opportunity to provoke them to ask questions and look at the story in a fresh way. For example, why is it so important that the angel came to Joseph?

Make your venue look like Christmas with decorations, background music and anything appropriately Christmassy! For some fun, you could play a party game at the beginning.

Why in

Being in small groups gives a chance for everyone to settle in, and also introduces the idea of Jesus in his family. Try one of these options:

ⓘ1 Family trees
(10 minutes)

Ask the children to draw their own family tree. Show a sample from your own family tree to explain how to do it. Don't include too many people, as the children will probably not know beyond their grandparents.

ⓘ2 Draw your home
(10 minutes)

Ask children to draw their home, including everyone who lives there. Draw your own home, making it fun by having people looking out of windows, doors, or even the chimney! Include any pets. If it's not a wonderful work of art, even better! It will encourage the children to have a go themselves. Invite the children to talk about their families.

Whys advice
Be prepared for any type of family in your group. Some of the children may live in very difficult or unhappy families, so may find this exercise hard. Invite the children to talk about their families. Some children fantasise about having fathers, or older brothers or sisters that they don't really have. Another child in the group may say, 'No, you haven't got a big sister!' Find time to talk with the child later. There may be all sorts of reasons why they invent such a person.

So, Why God?

ⓒ1 What does the Bible say?
(5 minutes)

Memory verse: Matthew 1:21
Tell the story of Joseph's dream from Matthew 1:19,20 as a background to understanding verse 21. Write Matthew 1:21 out on large pieces of paper or card, just one word or phrase per card. Children could hold them or use a Velcro display board. Show the whole verse and then remove a card, one at a time, while the children continue to repeat the verse (if you can say the verse to a rhythm, like a rap, this will help the children remember it better and make it more fun). You will need to explain how important names were in those days. Each one had a meaning. Jesus means 'the one who saves'.

ⓒ2 What's the story?
(15 minutes)

The Christmas story is so well known that you should be able to get the children to tell it to you. This should certainly get them all involved, as they will all know something about it. The key points that you want to emphasise are what Mary understood about Jesus from what she was told by:
• the angel
• the shepherds
• the wise men.
Don't lose sight of these points as you explore the story.

Build the storytelling around a game of pass the parcel. Photocopy the ten clues given on pages 14–15. Between each layer of wrapping, put a clue with a question, picture, puzzle or clue to prompt the children to 'unpack' the story. Keep asking the children to fill in the gaps, especially helping them to question the reason why things happened. Encourage them to wonder at the 'extraordinariness' of the Christmas story. Make sure that there is a prize for everyone in the final parcel, such as a sweet or an eraser.

ⓒ3 What's the answer?
(5 minutes)

Can the children answer this for themselves? Did any of the angels say anything that makes things clearer? If they need help, ask someone to read Matthew 1:24,25. (If you use the *Good News*

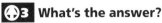

3

Bible, wait for the giggles! Children don't expect the Bible to mention the word 'sex'.)

If necessary, explain that it was God who made Mary pregnant, not Joseph, but Joseph no doubt played an important part in Jesus' life. Joseph probably taught Jesus to be a carpenter. Joseph obeyed God's commands given to him in dreams. We could say that Joseph was Jesus' stepfather. Explore the role of a stepfather, but be aware that for some children this may be their own experience. Some will be happy about this, others not so happy.

If the children want to talk further, look together at what the angel said to Mary in Luke 1:29–37.

Ask the children if they think Jesus worried about who his real father was. He certainly knew by the time he was twelve. If there is time, tell the story about Jesus in Jerusalem (Luke 2:41–50). Mary and Joseph probably told him as he grew up about the extraordinary events of his birth.

Whys advice

'The church needs children's evangelism like never before. For if it fails to engage with the generation now being born, the future is bleak.' *Children Finding Faith*, Francis Bridger (SU/CPAS, ISBN 1 85999 323 0)

So how can we help children know God? In this prize-winning book, Francis Bridger looks at the ways in which children develop physically, mentally and emotionally from birth to adolescence, and shows how these insights can help us to share the gospel more effectively with children.

Combining studies of child development with the author's own analysis of theological issues relating to children, *Children Finding Faith* is an important contribution to the ongoing discussion on child faith development. It is an essential read for those wanting to take seriously their work with children.

Why me?

①1 What can I do?
(20 minutes)

Make the most of the opportunity to talk as you work on one of the two options, **My Why Book!** or crafts.

Craft: mobiles

There are all sorts of mobiles that you can make. Many craft books have ideas. *Here's one I made earlier*, Kathyrn Copsey (SU) has a chapter on them. Make one yourself beforehand in order to help the children.

You will need:
- a wire coat hanger for each child
- tin foil, and perhaps some tinsel
- the artwork (on page 16) copied onto card
- coloured wool or silver thread.

Cover the coat hanger with tin foil, especially the sharp end. Colour each of the six drawings. Glitter pens and glue will make them more Christmassy. Punch a hole in each picture and attach each one to the coat hanger with thread. Use different lengths, but make sure the two end ones are the same length.

Whys advice

Don't store all the mobiles together. The strings get tangled very easily! Hang them on display until the children take them home.

①2 What now?
(5 minutes)

Pray together at the end of the group time. Thank God that Jesus came as a baby and that he knows what it is like to live on earth. You could sing an appropriate Christmas carol or listen to a Christmas song. Make sure the children have the words and talk about them before you sing. You may decide between you that some of the words are not true to what actually happened! (Carols are well known for getting the teaching about God wrong! Is it really true of Jesus that 'no crying he makes'?) The 'Calypso Carol' or 'Silent Night' would be suitable although even these contain some difficult ideas for children!

Postbox

Remind the children about the Postbox where they can put any questions they may have. You could give them all a Christmas card (out of season) with the memory verse written on it, which also thanks them for coming to **So, Why God?**

So, Who is God? **link**
Question 8 (page 34) could be useful for this topic as it refers to Jesus coming. Question 25 (page 90) explores Jesus as God.

Why did Jesus have to die?

Why4

Mark 14:53–64; 15:6–41;
Luke 23:36–47

Aims **To look at the reasons
for Jesus' death on the
cross.
To help children begin to
understand why Jesus had
to die.**

What's it all about?

There are at least two sides to Jesus' death:

Historical

Jesus died because the Jewish authorities feared that he was too popular (Luke 22:2) and might lead an uprising against the Romans (John 11:48).

The big picture

The reason Christians most commonly give for Jesus' death on the cross is that he died for us so that our sins could be forgiven, and our broken relationship with God could be put right. (Romans 5:9,10; 1 John 1:7; 4:10.)

What sort of leaders does Why4 need?

The subject of Jesus' death on the cross is not an easy one for leaders to share with children. Some children might be horrified at Jesus' crucifixion and so may fail to take in the real significance of Jesus' death.

The message of the cross is multifaceted and complex. Even the Bible writers stress different aspects of the cross. At the same time, it is a simple message. Look at 'Why does this question matter?' for understanding the cross in different ways.

We should help children respond appropriately to the message of the cross. By Why4, leaders have got to know their groups and will have a better understanding of each child's grasp of the gospel.

As with the Christmas story, please don't assume that you know the story so well that you won't need to read it again. Read the familiar Bible verses carefully in preparation, looking for fresh insights. Our minds can add details that are not actually there. For example was Jesus crucified on a green hill? Is that in the Bible, or is it just in the well known Easter hymn?

So, why does this question matter?

- God's ability to accept us and forgive our sin is dependent upon what Jesus did on the cross. This is at the heart of the gospel.
- God wants to have a relationship with us and to be our friend. But this friendship is spoilt by the wrong things we do, say and think, which the Bible sees as disobeying God – sin. No matter what we do, we cannot live in a way that pleases God. The punishment for sin is separation from God – death. However, God wants the opposite for us, a relationship with him – life!
- Jesus came to live on this earth as someone who was perfect, and died to take the punishment for our sin. God wants us to respond by accepting that Jesus has died in our place. We can turn back to God, to make a fresh start. The Bible calls this repentance.
- Children know all about trying to make a fresh start and failing, but God helps us when we start afresh with him. Our response must be one of repentance, turning back to God. It is more than being sorry, but that's a good start. It will eventually lead to a completely different focus to our lives.

As you prepare for this session, try to put the paragraphs above in your own words.

Understanding the cross in different ways

The explanation just given sees the cross as a work of substitution – Jesus died in our place. However the Bible presents other ways of seeing the cross that make sense to children. Here are two of them in case they help by explaining it another way:

JESUS THE VICTOR

Jesus' resurrection is a glorious demonstration that he has conquered evil and the final enemy, death (1 Corinthians 15:24–28). His victory will only be complete at the end of time, but we know for certain that he will be victorious. The story of Lazarus in John 11 is a story that children can grasp. They want to know who are the winners and the losers and to be reassured that evil will not win! The cross and resurrection are proof of this.

JESUS THE PEACEMAKER

Children know the consequences of broken relationships and the importance of making

4

peace. They will be aware of the search for peace in many regions in the world. Jesus, however, is the supreme example of someone who acted as a peacemaker sent by God to make peace between him and the human race. Mending broken relationships is important to children.

So, why do children ask, 'Why did Jesus have to die?'

- Most children will think that Jesus was a good man, who believed in his cause. In history they learn about people who were killed for what they believed. Is Jesus simply a martyr in the same vein as Joan of Arc or Martin Luther King – the innocent and good person who died unjustly?

- Did Jesus actually do something really awful that no one tells us about? We need to emphasise that Jesus never did anything wrong. His trial was a mockery, with witnesses who lied. He was only convicted on one count, and that was because he said he was the Son of God. Children are acutely aware of what is and is not just and fair, and so will understand the injustice of Jesus' death.

- For some children, the differences between right and wrong may be blurred. They may not know what they have done wrong. For others, there will be a genuine fear of doing wrong or of being caught doing wrong. (Is it all right to do wrong so long as you are not caught? Many streetwise kids would think so.) But all children will be aware that death is a serious punishment, so Jesus must have been accused of committing a serious crime!

- Children's television and literature are full of examples of the conflict between good and evil. Encourage children to comment on this during the discussion. Many will understand the feelings behind giving your life for others. They can identify with Jesus giving his life for others. It is worth reflecting on the sacrificial death of Simba's father in *The Lion King* or Ron Weasley's sacrifice in *Harry Potter and the Philosopher's Stone*.

- Expect discussion about Easter eggs and Easter bunnies. There is so much muddled thinking and ignorance about Good Friday and Easter!

Church children

Adults in church talk about Jesus' death, but don't necessarily explain what happened in child-friendly terms. For example, children are given the answer to 'Why did Jesus die on the cross?' as 'Jesus died to save us from our sins'. But what do they understand by this?

Why in

Welcome the children as they arrive. Don't mention the question for this So, Why God? during your groups, in case it interferes with one of the Why in activities. As you talk, look out for the various angles that are suggested in the section 'So, why do children ask...?'(above). In this session particularly, we must begin where the children are and with what they know. Try one of these alternatives:

1 The worst person ever
(10 minutes)

Ask the children to think of the worst person they can imagine. It might be a person from TV or a book, fictional or real, but not one they have made up themselves. Ask them to draw or write down why that person is the worst. For example, what have they done that makes them so bad? Next they should write down or draw the punishment that person should receive for being so awful. Be prepared for some terrible punishments!

2 Make the punishment fit
(10 minutes)

Ask the children to draw some punishments that might be used at school. Someone might steal their new pencil, or spoil their painting. Someone might hit them or not allow them to join in their game. What punishment should be given for these sorts of things? As a group, you could perhaps draw up a chart, putting various 'crimes' on different lines with the agreed punishment in the next column.

So, Why God?

1 What's the story?
(10 minutes)

Introduce the question, 'Why did Jesus have to die?' Reassure children that there may be more than one answer. Don't take any answers straight away, but ask them to try to answer the question once they have heard from someone who was there the day Jesus died.

Interview Barabbas

Ask an adult to pretend to be Barabbas and answer questions addressed to him by an interviewer. Simple dressing up adds to the effect. Barabbas' story comes in each of the gospels, eg Mark 15:6–15. Include the fact that Barabbas had murdered someone in a riot (Mark 15:7) which was punishable by death. Explain how he was set free. If you prefer, use the following drama script:

Interviewer: Hello, could you introduce yourself?
Barabbas: Certainly. My full name is Jesus Barabbas. My father was Abbas, and so I am Barabbas. It means 'Son of Abbas'. And I'm proud, but sometimes embarrassed, to have the same name as Jesus Christ.
Interviewer: Ah yes, I wanted to ask you about him.
Barabbas: I thought you might.
Interviewer: Why's that?
Barabbas: Well, everyone wants to know about him, and what really happened.
Interviewer: So what did happen?
Barabbas: Well, my parents brought me up as a good Jew. They did their best, but I gave them a hard time. I don't know how it happened really. I was fed up with the Romans in our country and wanted them driven out. I became an angry young man, and got involved with some others in planning to get rid of the Romans. All too quickly it went wrong. *(Pauses to sigh and mop his brow.)*
Interviewer: So you got caught up in violence?
Barabbas: Yes. I mean I had to defend myself! I had a knife and... *(Pauses.)*
Interviewer: Go on.
Barabbas: Well... in the middle of all the shouting and pushing, I stabbed a man. It was him or me. The Romans caught me just as I'd killed him. The punishment for a murderer is death. The Romans didn't think twice about putting me to death for what I'd done.
Interviewer: So that was why you were in prison that day, when Jesus Christ was on trial?
Barabbas: Yes, although I didn't know anything about Jesus. The governor, Pilate, just sent a couple of soldiers to collect a prisoner who'd done something awful. So they grabbed me, and took me to him. I think he wanted to set Jesus Christ free, but he gave the people a choice between Jesus Christ or me. I never thought I had a chance. All I knew about Jesus was that he was a good man who did good things. I'd killed a man.
Interviewer: But the crowd chose you!
Barabbas: I couldn't believe it, and I don't think

the governor could either. He turned to me, and told me I was free. He told the soldiers to let me go. I looked across at Jesus Christ before I went. I thought he would look angry or upset. He looked at me, and he wasn't angry or upset at all.
Interviewer: What a great story!
Barabbas: Yes, but the worst was still to come.
Interviewer: In what way?
Barabbas: Pilate, the governor, told the crowd that he thought Jesus was innocent, but it was up to them what he should do with him. I thought he was innocent as well, so I was stunned when I heard them shouting for him to be crucified. That was awful. He hadn't done anything wrong – he'd been good to people. And I was being set free. How can that be fair?

2 What's the answer?
(5 minutes)

Invite the children to ask Barabbas some questions, and then ask the question, 'Was it fair that Barabbas got off free, when he had killed someone?'
Further questions, if you need them:
• What should have happened to Barabbas?
• How does the story of Barabbas help to answer our question for today, 'Why did Jesus have to die?'

3 What does the Bible say?
(10 minutes)

The rest of the story is found in Mark 15:16–39; Luke 23:36–47
You will need:
• three cardboard crosses that can be stuck on a Velcro board
• two cards saying 'Done wrong'
• one card saying 'Nothing wrong'
• a card saying 'Crucify him!'

BEGINNING
(Hold up the 'Crucify him!' card at the right times.) Pilate asked the people again, 'What shall I do with Jesus?' And they shouted back, *(Children shout.)* 'Crucify him!' 'But what crime has he committed?' They shouted even louder, *(Children shout.)* 'Crucify him!' Pilate was a weak man, so he handed Jesus over to be crucified. *(Explain how the soldiers mocked Jesus, then led him away to the Place of a Skull. Read Mark 15:16–22.)*

MAIN POINT
The soldiers banged nails through Jesus' hands and feet, and nailed him to a rough piece of

4

wood. This wasn't like the smooth crosses you see in churches; it was a rough piece of tree trunk. Then they put up the cross between two criminals, who were also being crucified. *(Stick the three crosses onto the Velcro board and put the 'Nothing wrong' card over the middle cross.)*

People came by and they mocked Jesus. Listen to how Luke described it. *(Read Luke 23:32–43.)* Even one of the criminals being crucified with Jesus mocked him. The other criminal tried to stop him, telling him that they had both done wrong things and deserved to be crucified. *(Put the 'Done wrong' cards on each of the outer crosses.)* This criminal turned to Jesus and said, 'Remember me, Jesus, when you come as King.' Jesus promised him that he would be in paradise with him that day. As Jesus died, all the things the criminal had done were put onto Jesus, and when God looked down on that scene, it was as if the criminal had never done anything wrong. *(Swap over the card from one outer cross with that on Jesus' cross.)*

ENDING

The blame for the criminal's sins was taken from him and put on Jesus. In the same way, the wrong things we have said or done, things that have spoiled our relationship with God, can be taken from us and put on Jesus. If we want this for ourselves, and want to be forgiven, we need to be sorry and really want to be a friend of God. It's a sad story, but it doesn't end there because Jesus didn't stay dead. He came alive again. You'll hear the rest of the story next time.

You may feel it appropriate to invite the children to talk with God about this, thanking him for Jesus' death and asking to be forgiven. You may like to photocopy and use the prayer card on page 17. This sort of prayer has helped lots of children to respond to God. It is important to tell the children that they don't have to use a prayer someone else has written – they can say what they really feel to God. It's just that the prayer card may help them express what they want to say.

Why me?

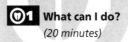 **What can I do?**
(20 minutes)

In your groups, remember the things you have talked about so far and try to relate the activities to them – the craft or **My Why Book!**.

Craft: sun catchers

You will need:

- black card, cut in advance if necessary
- white and coloured tissue paper
- glue sticks

Cut a piece of black card approximately 15 cm x 10 cm. Fold in half, and cut out half a cross shape along the middle of the fold, so that you have a cross-shaped hole in the middle when you open it out. Stick a piece of thin white tissue paper over the back of the black card, and stick little pieces of coloured tissue paper on it, or try a mosaic style with little pieces. (Alternatively, use tracing paper to back the card and colour the paper using brightly coloured felt-tip pens.)

The sun catcher can be stuck or hung in a window.

We did this

We cut our black card in a church window shape. We used a glue pen to put glue onto the white tissue paper and then stuck the coloured tissue onto that.

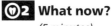 **What now?**
(5 minutes)

At the end of the group time, pray together. Thank God that Jesus came to die for us, and that he forgives us. Some children may be happy to write or say sorry prayers very openly. Be sure to involve the children in the prayers as before.

Bring in a rough piece of wood or some sharp nails to put in the middle of the circle as you pray. Let the children touch them (but be careful about splinters and sharp points). This will help them realise something of the horror of Jesus' death. Let the children look at this wood or nails as you pray.

Postbox

Don't forget the Postbox, with a chance for the children to write more questions. Arrange for a leader to go 'On the spot' next time, to answer any questions already posted, and maybe to give their testimony.

How did Jesus come back to life?

Why5

Mark 16:1–8; John
14:16,23–26; 20:1–8;
Ephesians 1:19,20

Aims **To make sure the
children know that Jesus
came back to life, and
that he is alive now.
To think about God's
great power in making
the resurrection possible.**

What's it all about?

Jesus was raised from the dead

Many children know that Jesus died on a cross,
but far fewer will realise that he came back to
life and is still alive today. We want to share the
amazing stories of Jesus' resurrection and his
ascension to heaven. Soon after Jesus left, the
Holy Spirit came to be with us. By giving the
whole story, we help children to understand how
Jesus is alive today and can be our friend.

God's great power

If God could make everything by just saying a
word, then we shouldn't really be surprised that
his power could raise Jesus from the dead. This
same power is available to help us in our lives
and to give us the eternal life that Jesus
promised.

What sort of leaders does Why5 need?

Leaders should have a clear picture of events to
enable the children to see the whole story from
the resurrection onwards. Tell the story briefly,
picking up on what they already know, but
filling in any gaps. Leaders need to be flexible
and prepared to go with the children's questions
and input.

Children may have already begun to respond
to Jesus. Some may have asked for a prayer card
in the last session, whilst others may say they are
Christians already. Leaders need to be open to
help them, but be careful not to pressurise them
into making a decision they are not ready for, or
that they do not really understand.

The resurrection accounts in the four Gospels
are all different. They are four different portraits
of the same person by different artists. Read all
four versions in preparation for this session.
Think about how the differences in the four
accounts are evidence that this wasn't a false
story made up by the disciples. If they had done
that, they would have done a much better job in
ironing out the apparent discrepancies! As a
group of leaders, use your Bibles to work out
exactly what did happen.

Whys advice

Look for helpful background on this story in the
book written by Frank Morison, a lawyer, who
set out to disprove the resurrection. After
examining alternative explanations for Jesus'
empty tomb, he ended up writing, *Who moved
the stone?* (Faber and Faber), in which he
explains how Jesus must have come back to life.
This is the only explanation that fits the facts, he
said. For more detailed evidence concerning the
resurrection, read *Evidence that demands a
verdict* by Josh McDowell (Alpha).

So, why does this question matter?

The truth of the resurrection is the foundation of
our faith. Paul says in 1 Corinthians 15:14, 'And if
Christ wasn't raised to life, our message is
worthless, and so is your faith.' Paul said this in
the context of proving that the dead will rise to
life. The two are linked together. We believe in
eternal life and that we will go to be with God
when we die. This belief depends on the truth
that God raised Christ to life. Jesus' resurrection
demonstrated God's power to do the same for
us: 'He makes us certain that others will also be
raised to life' (1 Corinthians 15:20).

The fact that God raised Jesus to life shows
that he accepted the sacrifice of Jesus' death for
our forgiveness. The resurrection shows that
Jesus is the Lord of life and has the right to offer
us eternal life. On the day of Pentecost, Peter
said, 'Death could not hold him in its power'
(Acts 2:24).

As the resurrection is so central to the
Christian faith, many people have put forward
alternative explanations for the empty tomb. It's
worth thinking about some of these:

JESUS' FRIENDS TOOK THE BODY/THEY WERE
HALLUCINATING
Jesus' friends were petrified when Jesus was
arrested. Many years later, most of these same
people were killed for believing that Jesus rose
from the dead. Would they really die for what
they knew was a lie? It is unlikely that five
hundred people would all have the same
hallucination (1 Corinthians 15:6).

5

THE JEWISH LEADERS TOOK THE BODY
If this were true, the Jewish leaders would have only had to produce the body when Jesus' friends started to preach about his resurrection, and they would have destroyed the rumour. Why would they want to remove the body anyway?

JESUS' FRIENDS WENT TO THE WRONG TOMB
Jesus' friends included the person who owned the tomb, so although an initial mistake was possible, it would have come to light very quickly. Furthermore, the Jewish leaders knew the right tomb and would have quickly pointed out the error.

So, why do children ask, 'How did Jesus come back to life?'

- Children experience death in different ways: a well loved pet, a grandparent or more distant relative or neighbour. A few children will experience the death of a parent or a close friend. They may well be told that the person has gone to be with Jesus, or with the angels in heaven. Death is never easy for any of us, but the possibility of life after death is of great comfort to us all, including children.

- For children who don't truly realise that Jesus is alive today, it can be hard to understand how Christians can talk about Jesus as their friend now. They may even have heard about Jesus coming back to life, but assume that he went on to die again. After all, he's not around on earth for them to see today. Introducing the Holy Spirit helps to explain how God is with us, even though we can't see him.

- Children who have had to face up to death may eventually be told that they won't see the person (or animal) again on this earth. They can't come back to life again on earth, even though the child may be told that the person is with Jesus. So if people and animals don't come back to life on earth, how could Jesus have done so?

- Children love ghost stories! Some may even claim to have seen a ghost. It is important to establish that Jesus was not a ghost. They may be interested in the exact description of Jesus' resurrected body. (He could eat, make a fire, walk and talk, but he could walk through doors and disappear without warning. His disciples knew who he was, but Cleopas didn't immediately recognise him.) Look at what children are currently reading or watching about ghosts and spiritual beings, to be in touch with their thinking.

- Someone who came back to life after a crucifixion must have had lots of power at his disposal. Children in films see all sorts of expressions of power achieving the impossible, both good and bad. They welcome any explanation of the resurrection which says it was God's power which raised Jesus from the dead (Ephesians 1:19,20.) See the reference to Jesus the Victor in Why4 (page 33).

Church children

Those who have been brought up in Christian families should know the facts of the Easter story. Surprisingly, many often don't know the rest of Jesus' life on earth, except that he went up to heaven. They may have heard of the Holy Spirit but, depending on the church they attend, will have had varying emphases placed upon his role.

Whys advice

If you want to be ready to help children who have experienced the death of a close relative or friend, *The Strong Tower*, by Robert Harrison (SU), is a useful tool.

Why in

◖1 Planting Seeds
(10 minutes)

Lay out a selection of seeds in numbered plastic transparent bags. Put the pictures from the packets (or a book) in another row and letter them. Children should try to guess which plants will grow from which seed, matching the numbers with the letters. Include a good variety – in fact anything that can cause something to grow. Mustard seeds are very tiny. Broad beans are themselves the seeds for the plant. Bring in a conker or an acorn. If you plant one, a great tree will grow. Get the children to talk about their answers in pairs, and then discuss them altogether, with the leader finally showing the correct picture for each seed. Take the conker as an example. What happens to its beautiful shiny skin when you plant it? What do you get if it really grows well?

So, Why God?

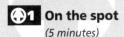

☺1 On the spot
(5 minutes)

Put a leader 'On the spot' to answer questions. Read out any jokes or show pictures from the Postbox to get started. Then move on to appropriate questions from the Postbox. In addition, ask about the leader's personal faith: 'Why do you believe in God?' 'When did you start to believe in God?' 'How often do you talk to Jesus?'

☺2 What does the Bible say?
(5 minutes)

Ask half the children to imagine they are the angel/the young man in white inside the tomb. The rest of the children are to be Mary Magdalene. Give them each a piece of paper and a pencil. Ask them to write down, or draw, what they would have felt and seen as the angel or Mary on the day Jesus rose from death, as you read them Mark 16:1–8 and John 20:1–18.

Whys advice

There is a powerful episode at the end of *The Tanglewoods' Secret* by Patricia St John (SU). Mr Tandy uses the example of a conker to help a child, Ruth, understand death and resurrection. Ruth was upset because they had just buried her friend, Terry. It didn't seem like he had gone to heaven to be with Jesus like everyone had said. You could read that part of the book to help children with similar uncertainty.

☺3 What's the story?
(10 minutes)

Jesus' friends meet him again.

BEGINNING
Talk about what the children have put on their pieces of paper. Try to capture the wonder of the occasion and the human emotion.

MAIN POINT
Emphasise the fact that Jesus did come back to life. Can the children remember any other stories about people he met after this? You may need to focus upon only one. They are all listed here for completeness:
- The two disciples on the road to Emmaus (Luke 24:13–35 – we will look at this in more depth in Why6).

- Jesus appeared to his friends and ate some fish with them (Luke 24:36–44).
- Thomas doubted Jesus was alive, but believed when he saw Jesus (John 20:24–29).
- Jesus' friends went fishing, Jesus set up a barbecue on the beach (John 21:1–14).
- Jesus went up the mountain and told his friends what they must do (Matthew 28:16–20).
- Jesus went up to heaven (Luke 24:50–53).

ENDING
End with two final things about this time in the life of Jesus:
- The angel in Acts 1:11 said that Jesus will come back again in the same way. He can only come back if he is still alive. Acts 1:9 says he was taken up to heaven and that's where he still is, alive with God.
- In Matthew 28:20, Jesus' last words to his friends were that he would be with them always. Yet he went to heaven soon after. Jesus promised to send the Holy Spirit, who would stay with them forever (John 14:16). We can't see the Holy Spirit, but he is with everyone who is Jesus' friend, wherever they are.

☺4 What's the answer?
(5 minutes)

The question has already been answered, but some children may still want to know the significance of this new body and how the resurrection happened. After all, it is humanly impossible for anyone to come back to life! That is exactly the point. Humanly it is impossible. Look up Ephesians 1:19,20. Paul wrote these words to followers of Jesus in a city called Ephesus. His purpose in writing was to demonstrate God's great power, not specifically to discuss the resurrection. He writes that the resurrection was possible because God's power can do amazing things. Jesus' new body was evidence of God's power, evidence that when we die it is not the end. Those who love Jesus will be given a new body, one that will last for ever. Jesus' new body gives us some clues as to what that body will be like. Wow! 1 Corinthians 15 gives us lots more clues about the resurrection, but it is hard to unpack this with a group of children. This is an opportunity to talk about heaven if the children are showing interest.

THE HOLY SPIRIT
It is important that you end with an explanation of who the Holy Spirit is and what he does now. Read to the children John 14:16,17,26. Jesus told

5

the disciples that the Holy Spirit would come. He said God the Father would send another helper like himself. So the Holy Spirit is the same as Jesus. Look at these verses again and talk about what the Holy Spirit does now. You could do this by photocopying the puzzle below, or making an acetate to use on an OHP.

Use the Bible verses to work out the missing words in these sentences. They all contain an H, an S or a T.

The Father s____ the H___ S_____ who will be with you _____s.
The S_____ will h___ you.
He will s_____ you what is t_____.
The S_____ will come in the place of __s_s.
The S_____ will t_____ you everything and remind you what __s_s t____ you.

Share how the Holy Spirit helps you and reminds you about what Jesus said. We will return to think more about the Holy Spirit in Why9.

Why me?

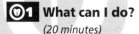

⑦1 What can I do?
(20 minutes)

Encourage your group to talk further or ask more questions about Jesus' coming back to life and going to heaven. Use the craft or **My Why Book!**.

Craft: Newspapers
You will need:
• a large sheet of paper for each group
• white paper
• old newspapers
• glue and child-safe scissors
• pencils and felt-tip pens

Make a group newspaper report of the first Easter Sunday, including headlines, a photograph or picture, a report of the events, interviews with witnesses, adverts (eg camel trips to the Dead Sea, Chariots for hire, Best Quality Spices) and any other features the children can suggest. You will need to use Bibles to check the details.

Children can all work around the large sheet, or produce their contributions on a single smaller sheet of paper which is then stuck onto the large sheet. Use old newspapers for ideas, and to cut out large print words or letters for headlines.

Alternatively, a small group might like to make a radio news bulletin reporting the event with added adverts. Older children love making recordings on tape or computer. You will need to bring in music or sound effects that they can use for their programme.

We did this
'After grasping how God made the world, no one had any problem with God raising Jesus from the dead. In fact when I asked how it happened, one of the older girls simply said, 'God did it!' We always pray for the right ways to say things and God always puts the words in our mouths. Sometimes I feel I'm there listening to myself... wondering where the fluency comes from!'

⑦1 What now?
(5 minutes)

At the end of the group time, pray together. Thank Jesus that we can know he is alive. Remind the children of what you talked about last week – saying sorry for what we have done wrong. Thank Jesus for the promise that the Holy Spirit will always be with us. Ask that the children will experience more of him in their lives. You could put this prayer on an acetate and ask the children to join in the phrases in bold:

Jesus, we have so much to thank you for.
Thank you, Jesus, that you are alive!
You came as a baby to this world. You know what it is like to be a human being.
Thank you, Jesus, that you are alive!
You made so many friends and cared for so many people.
Thank you, Jesus, that you are alive!
You chose to die a painful death. But that was not the end! So we can say...
Thank you, Jesus, that you are alive!
And once you had gone to heaven, you sent the Holy Spirit to be with us forever.
Thank you, Jesus, that you are alive!
Holy Spirit, thank you that you are with us forever. Amen.

Postbox
Remind the children to put questions in the Postbox. If 'On the spot' went well, tell the children who will be the leader 'On the spot' at the next session. They could then write specific questions for that person.

How do we know the Bible is true?

What's it all about?
God's message to us

Christians believe that God is a communicating God. We have already seen how he communicates through creation and his Son. This session we will concentrate on his words and, to a lesser extent, his people. The Bible is vital to our Christian faith, and we believe it to be true. Just as it is impossible to prove absolutely the existence of God, so it is impossible to prove that the Bible is true. However, just as we can use evidence to help us believe in God, so there is evidence that can help us believe that the Bible is God's reliable Word for us.

Discovering the meaning of the Bible

The only real way to make up your mind about the Bible is to read it for yourself. Historical evidence points towards the reliability of the Bible, but unless we let the Bible speak to us it remains a dull old book full of dry facts. We want to encourage children to look into the Bible for themselves and discover the wonders that are there for everyone.

The Bible was written for God's people by about forty different authors over a period of about 1,600 years. In trying to understand any part of it, we need to think about who wrote it, who they were writing for and what was going on at the time. The Bible contains several different types of writing, such as history, poetry, prophecy and letters. The type of writing may affect how we understand it.

What sort of leaders does Why6 need?

Leaders who love the Bible: the children will have already worked out what we think about the Bible. If we are constantly referring to it to help answer their questions and speak warmly about how God has spoken to us, they will see how important the Bible is.

Leaders who respect the Bible: the Bible is not a lucky charm to carry with us so that things will go well. It is not a book to dip into for instant

'blessed thoughts'. Nor should we use it to prove our pet theories by quoting verses out of context. To use the Bible properly we need time and effort to get to know it better.

Leaders who practise hearing from God as they read the Bible: it is difficult to encourage children to read the Bible and hear God's message if we are not doing this ourselves.

It would be great if the children could hear how God has recently spoken to each of the leaders in various ways, including through the Bible.

So, why does this question matter?

Few people today believe in absolute truths as traditionally understood, so few people are interested in whether the Bible is true or not. What matters, people say, is whether it works for you. Actually, Christianity does work, but that is not what makes it true. It works because it is true: it is not true just because it works!

Long after you have moved on from the lives of these children, if they have been left with a love for the Bible, you will have enabled them to go on knowing God and maturing in their faith. Children need to be taught how to read the Bible. It was not originally written for children, and is a challenge to read.

What do children need to know?

- Children need to discover where to find books in the Bible (by using the contents page or by being given page numbers). Explaining that there are two parts/testaments is an important place to start.
- Chapter and verse divisions need to be explained.
- Not all parts of the Bible are stories, eg letters contain instructions; poetry and prophecy often look different on the page and use picture language.
- The Bible is not a handbook of instructions but a collection of different types of books. The two key questions to keep on asking are: What does this tell me about God? What does this show me about how God wants me to live?

Why6

Luke 24:13–32

Aims **To realise that God speaks to us in lots of ways: through the world he has made; through the Son he has sent; through the book he has given and through the people who know him.**
To consider especially the Bible as God's message to us.
To show children how to read the Bible for themselves, and to discover that God speaks to us today as we read it.

6

- There are a number of good child-friendly versions of the Bible available, but the different versions can be confusing, so stick to one when you are working with the children, preferably one that they can use themselves.
- Children need to be gradually introduced to the skills of handling the Bible. The main reason for doing this is to make it possible for them to hear from God themselves – both now and throughout their lives. The most valuable legacy any children's worker can leave with a child is a love for the Bible, with the expectation that God can and will speak to them. Knowing the skills to help them read it for themselves will make this possible.

Whys advice
Further reading for leaders:
The Story of the Book (SU) Terence Copley.
The Bible as History (Bantam) Werner Keller is excellent on archaeological digs and what they have found.
Evidence that demands a verdict (Alpha/Scripture Press) Josh McDowell contains a massive collection of evidence for the Christian faith, and a good chapter on the reliability of the Bible, including comparisons with other ancient texts.
Light to Live By (SU) Richard Briggs.
Understanding the Bible (SU) John Stott.
The Adventure Begins (SU/CPAS) by Terry Clutterham is a fantastic resource book for children's work and full of ideas about helping children read the Bible.
Children's Guide to the Bible (SU) by Robert Willoughby is an invaluable tool for helping children grasp the whole Bible story from Genesis to Revelation.

So, why do children ask, 'How do we know the Bible is true?'
We get our answers from the Bible
In practice, over the last few sessions, we have frequently been referring to the Bible, so some children will naturally ask how we know it is true.
Children are sorting out fact and fantasy
Around the ages of 7 to 11, children are working out what is real and what is make-believe. In order to do this they look for proof that things are true. Being told something by parents or even teachers is not enough for them any more. They want to know why they should believe it. This attitude is a good one and not to be feared. We should help them to explore different ways of discovering what is really true.
Sacred religious texts
In Religious Education lessons at school, children will have encountered the scriptures of other world religions. Are they all equally valid? Christians believe that the authority of the Bible makes it stand out as a unique book with a unique stamp of God's authority.

Church children
Church children may be overfamiliar with Bible stories. By the time they are 9 or 10 many are beginning to question what they have been taught. This is a natural, healthy process and should be encouraged.

Church children can help in our group if they are encouraged to share what they know about the Bible with others. They may have experience of when the Bible has helped them or their families.

Why in

Choose one of these activities to get your group started:

(I)1 Sign language
(10 minutes)

Divide the children into pairs as they arrive and give them different sentences or Bible verses. They need to work out their own sign language to communicate their message to the other groups.

(I)2 Drawing on backs
(10 minutes)

Sit your small groups in a line, preferably on the floor, each child facing the back of the one in front. Whisper the name of an object to the child at the end (or have it drawn on a card that you can show them). They have to draw this on the back of the person in front, using their finger. Ask them to be gentle! This person then has to draw with their finger on the back of the person in front of them, and so on, until the person at the front has to say what they think the object is. (To add a competitive element, one group could race another with the same object, the winner being the first to get it correctly to the front.) Use very simple things – a circle, square, house, cloud, sun, cross etc.

So, Why God?

⊕1 What do you know?
(25 minutes)

If 'On the spot' worked well last time, the children may like to question another leader. As this session is about the Bible, and on how God has spoken more generally in creation, include questions about how the person knows God speaks, how they read the Bible, why they think it can be trusted, and their favourite verse, Bible story or character.

If children don't seem to want to ask questions, devise a quiz on the whole of the first half of **So, Why God?** as a good way of reviewing the course so far.

Quiz
Suggested questions based on **So, Why God?**
Why1: What does God look like?
What strange thing did Moses see when he met God? (A bush that was on fire but wasn't burning up.)
What did Moses have to do when he came near the bush? (Take his sandals off, because God is holy.)
Why2: How did God make people?
Can you remember how God made people? (He made a man out of soil and breathed life into him.)
God looked for a friend for the first man – who or what was right as a friend? (The first woman.)
Why3: Who was Jesus' real Dad, Joseph or God?
(God; Joseph was more like his stepfather.)
What verse did we learn about Jesus when he was born? (Matthew 1:21)
Why4: Why did Jesus have to die?
Who got let off when Jesus died? (Barabbas, or the criminal on the cross, or all of us!)
What did Jesus do wrong so that they killed him? (Trick question! Nothing, although they accused him of blasphemy.)
Why5: How did Jesus come back to life?
What were the women worried about when they were on their way to the grave? (How to move the stone.)
How could Jesus possibly come back to life after he died? (By God's great power.)

⊕2 What does the Bible say?
(15 minutes)

The Emmaus Road story
Last session we looked at Jesus' resurrection and what happened after that. This session we will look at one event in depth and explore the Bible verses from Luke 24. It is essential for all children to have a Bible, or to enlarge the Bible verses onto an OHP acetate and use that.
To help the children make sense of this story you will need six outline pictures as shown on page 18. If you are using an OHP, put the pictures onto acetate, or use a large sheet of paper. Children can follow the Bible verses (probably read by a leader since this is a long story). Add the facial expressions and put in your own words what people are saying, in the speech bubbles with felt-tip pens. 1 – verses 13–14; 2 – verses 15-18; 3 – verses 19,20; 4 – verses 25–27; 5 – verses 28,29; 6 – verses 30-32.

WORK IT OUT FOR YOURSELVES
- Who is the story about? What do we know about the characters? (vs 13,15,18)
- Are they happy or sad? Why? (vs 17,19–24)
- Why do you think they didn't recognise Jesus? (vs 15,16)
- What did Jesus do that helped them to recognise him? (v 30)
- Jesus helped to solve his friends' problem. What does this say to us, if we are his friends today?
- How did Jesus help them to understand he was the Messiah? (You will need to explain that 'the Scriptures' meant the Old Testament.)
- Why do you think Jesus used the Scriptures? What does that say to us about the Bible? (This is the crucial question in this session. Jesus saw his own life and death in terms of what had been foretold in the Bible. He then used the Old Testament because he trusted it.)

⊕3 What's the answer?
(5 minutes)

Explain that as with lots of things about God, we can't prove completely that the Bible is true but that there has been a lot of historical evidence to suggest it is. Say that the best way to find out more about the Bible is to read it and to ask God to speak to them through it. Ask each leader

6

(give them one minute only) to tell everyone about a recent time that God has spoken to them through the Bible. The relevance and reality of the Bible to them personally will communicate to the children. Be sure that the leaders have been warned, to save embarrassment or rambling! If they are not sure how to talk about the Bible, suggest they read one or two verses, and explain why this is important to them, or what they think God is saying to them as they read it.

Why me?

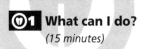 **What can I do?**
(15 minutes)

As this is the last group time of this half of So, Why God?, we want to equip children to be able to go on reading the Bible for themselves and to go on hearing from God, especially if you are having a break before doing the second half.

Start Snapshots through Mark

You will need a copy of *Snapshots through Mark* for each child in your group, available from SU.

Today's group time is deliberately shorter. Hand out *Snapshots through Mark*, and ask the children to write their names on page 1. Explain that it is called *Snapshots* because it is the size of a photo, and it helps children to take a snapshot of a small piece of the Bible each day. Its size makes it easy to carry around.

Explain that in *Snapshots through Mark* most of the Bible verses are printed so they don't have to find them in a Bible. If they can find them in their own Bible, suggest they do that as well. Work through the first day together, then let the children have a go at working through the second day on their own.

Ask the children what they should talk with God about using the 'Talk with God' suggestions on Days 1 and 2. See if one or more of the children would like to say a prayer about this and if others would like to pray about different things.

Carrying on with Snapshots through Mark

Tell the children they can take *Snapshots through Mark* with them, to carry on with what they have learnt in **So, Why God?** even though the first part of the course has finished. Explain briefly how to do the next day. Suggest they bring their *Snapshots through Mark* to show you at a suitable time (perhaps in church or in school), so that you can see how they are getting on. Encourage them to finish it before you start the second half of **So, Why God?** Make sure they know when you are going to run the second half.

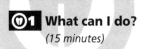 **What now?**
(10 minutes)

It is important to finish off this half of *So, Why God?* properly. Don't let anyone be too sad, not even the leaders! Highlight other things they can come to at church or school. Maybe you could offer to answer more questions if they write them down and send them to you. Make sure everyone takes home their books and any craft not yet claimed. Finish with a final prayer together with everyone holding hands. Use a Bible blessing such as 2 Corinthians 13:14 NIV (the grace) or Numbers 6:24–26 (the Aaronic blessing).

> May the LORD bless you and take care of you;
> May the LORD be kind and gracious to you;
> May the LORD look on you with favour and give you peace.
>
> **Numbers 6:24–26 (Good News)**

And finally...

If you are having a family evening, parents' time or party to finish this half of **So, Why God?** don't forget to tell children and parents about it. (See 'How to finish each half of **So, Why God?** for details of these events. Page 10.)

What did the angel tell Joseph to do? (verse 24)

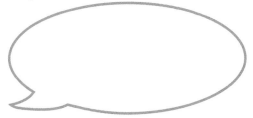

Did he do it? Yes/No

It must have been hard for Joseph to obey the angel, but it must have been even harder to believe what the angel said!

How would you have felt if you had been Joseph?

_____

_____

Was he really pleased? Yes/No

Was he worried? Yes/No

Tell God what you have talked about. Ask him to help you understand what happened when Jesus was born.

Read **Luke 2:41–50** to find out more about Jesus as a boy and Joseph as a dad.

How old was Jesus?

Where did he go?

Who went with him?

Where did he end up?

What do you think Joseph made of all this?

Look back to the things you wrote about a real dad on page 9. In what ways was Joseph Jesus' dad? In what ways was God Jesus' dad? Fill in this chart.

Joseph	God

My Why Book Challenge

God wanted a suitable friend for Adam. Some versions of the Bible say he needed a 'companion', others say a 'helper', and others say a 'partner'. Choose one of these words and see how many smaller words you can get out of them. Here are some to get you started...

COMPANION –   PAN MAN CAN NAP

Psst! Look back to page 4. What other signs for God's character can you make up from today's So Why God?

Why did Jesus have to die?

This is such a sad story. It all seems so unfair.

Talk about what you felt as you heard the story. Circle any of the words here if they are right for you. In the spaces, write in any extra words.

Sad upset angry _____

Not fair ____ worried pity

Disappointed _____ why? love

Read the first part of the story in **Mark 15:7–11.**

Try to answer the questions.

What had Barabbas done? _____

What should his punishment have been?

_____

Why was he let off? _____

_____

Was it fair? _____

How would Joseph answer today's question?

How would Mary answer today's question?

How would Jesus answer today's question?

How do you answer today's question?

Can you spot eight differences between the two pictures of Jesus in the Temple?

Who was Jesus' real Dad: God or Joseph?

Before you read the Bible, talk about what makes a real dad. Write down five favourite things a dad does. Of course, mums do lots of these things too.

A dad

_____

_____

_____

_____

Read **Matthew 1:18–25** (Matthew is the first book in the New Testament, the second part of the Bible.) Write down five things that these verses tell us about Joseph.

Joseph was

_____

_____

_____

_____

Think of a time when you did something wrong.

Did you get punished?

Did you get let off?

Was it fair?

How do you feel if you get blamed for something you haven't done?

Read the next part of the story in **Mark 15:16–18** and finish off the picture.

Imagine a world without any other people. You are all alone with just the animals and birds. That's what it was like for Adam.

God cares so much, that he doesn't want us to be alone. He made girls and boys, who are all different – tall and short, quiet and noisy, sport-loving, musical, talkative...
What other differences can you think of?

We don't know exactly how God made people, but we do know he was very pleased with what he had done.

God has specially made us, and he has made us to be with other people, so we are not alone. Write a message to God, telling him how you feel.

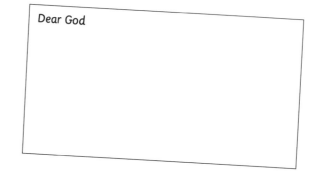

Dear God

Why 2

Let's read what we heard earlier from the Bible.

Read **Genesis 2:18–23**. Use the Bible verses to answer the crossword. (You will need Genesis 1:24 to answer question 3)

2 God didn't want the man to be_ _ _ _ _.

3 God made_ _ _ _ _ _ _and birds on the sixth day.

4 But still there was nothing that made a _ _ _ _ _ _ _ _friend.

5 The man gave all the animals and birds a_ _ _ _.

1 What God made to be a friend for Adam.

Why 4

Read **Mark 15:19–24.**
How many other terrible things were done to Jesus? But something even worse than all that happened! What did Jesus cry out? Look at Mark 15:34. You can either write in Aramaic, which is the language that Jesus spoke, or you can write in English.

Why did God abandon Jesus? This was bad news for Jesus but it is good news for us.
Can you think why?

Why 1

We have discovered what God is like, even though we haven't got a very clear picture of what he looks like. Work out some signs with your hands to help you remember some characteristics of God.

GOD IS LIKE A FLAME/FIRE.
GOD SPEAKS. GOD IS HOLY.
GOD LISTENS. GOD RESCUES.
GOD HAS ALWAYS BEEN AND ALWAYS WILL BE. HE IS ETERNAL.

At the start of **So, Why God?** you drew a picture of God. Would you draw something different now? Draw another picture of God in the frame below.

Talk with God about what you have found out about him. Write down what you want to say, or draw it, or just say it out loud. Everyone else can say, "Amen" which means, "I agree with that!"

Why 5

How did Jesus come back to life?

The sad story of Jesus' death has a happy ending. Draw a snapshot to show where they put Jesus' body.

Why 4

Several extraordinary things happened when Jesus died. Read **Matthew 27:45–54** then draw one of these things.

Ask your leader what this means. Can you work out why the curtain ripped "rom top to bottom"?
Can you say this prayer?

> Thank you Jesus that you love me.
> Thank you Jesus that you suffered so much pain for me.
> Thank you Jesus that you died for me.

Why 2

How did God make people?

You will have listened to **Genesis 2:4–7** already. Now read it for yourself.

Read **Genesis 2:4–7** (Genesis is the first book in the Bible). Put verse 7 in your own words.

_____

_____

How does it make you feel when you hear that God made people in this special way? Write down two words that describe the way you feel.

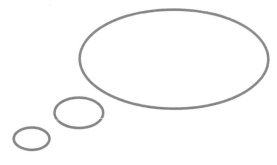

Why 5

Here's the happy ending!
Read **John 20:11–18**.
Find all these words from the verses in the wordsearch, then use the missing letters to finish off this sentence.

Mary went and told the_ _ _ _ _ _ _ _ _ what Jesus had told her.

D	I	C	S	T	I	C	I
G	A	R	D	E	N	E	R
B	N	Y	T	A	O	T	E
O	G	I	O	C	B	I	H
D	E	N	M	H	B	H	T
Y	L	G	B	E	A	W	A
P	S	L	E	R	R	S	F

TOMB, ANGELS, GARDENER, CRYING, FATHER, WHITE, BODY, TEACHER, RABBONI

Why 1

Read Exodus 3:9–15.
Verses 9 and 10 tell us something really great about God. Cross out every X, Y and Z to find out.

GXOZZDHEYAYRXDYTHZXECRZXEYSOXFHZXYSPEOX
YPZLXZE.GOZXDCAXMEYXTZOTYZXHZERXZEXSYCZU
YEXOYZFZHXISXPYEZOPXZLEX.

_____

_____

God still listens to us when we ask him to help us. While Moses was talking with God, he asked God his name (verse 13). What was the answer (verse 14)?
What does God's name tell us about God?
What does this mean?

_____

Why 1

What did the Lord say when Moses came near the bush? Look at verse 4.

What did Moses reply?

God talked to a person, just as we talk with our friends. What's more, God talked to Moses, even though he was murderer.

What else can you find out about God in verses 5 and 6?

Talk about why you think Moses was afraid. What does that say about God?

Psst! God is sometimes called the Lord.

Psst! Being holy means that God is very pure and powerful. He cannot stand bad things.

Why 5

Talk about how Mary felt going to the tomb. How would her feelings have changed? Draw the expression on Mary's face as her feelings change

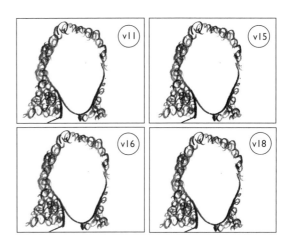

Write down all you know about Jesus' new body...

_____
_____
_____

Welcome to **My Why Book!** It will help you to look at what the Bible says in answer to the questions in the **So Why God?** course. Not every question has an easy answer, but you'll have found an answer to most of the questions by the end!

You should be able to work through **My Why Book!** on your own, but if you need some help, ask your group leader.

Here are the **So Why God?** questions that you will be thinking about over the next few weeks.

What does God look like?

How did God make people?

Who was Jesus' real dad: God or Joseph?

Why did Jesus have to die?

How did Jesus come back to life?

How do we know the Bible is true?
(Question 6 is not answered in **My Why Book!**)

We hope you find lots of answers!

Why 5

The leaders of **So, Why God?** are

_____
_____

What I have learnt about God

_____
_____
_____

One question that still needs an answer

_____
_____

What I am going to do after **So, Why God?**

_____

My friends at **So, Why God?** are

_____
_____

Get them to sign their names on the back of the booklet.

But there is more to this story. Who was it who made it possible for Jesus to come alive again?

Because Jesus is still alive, he has shown that there is life beyond death for everyone who believes in Jesus.

How do you know that Jesus is still alive?

Is it important that Jesus is alive today? Write down your thoughts in the bubble.

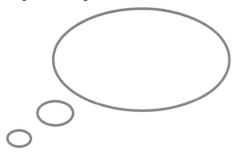

Tell God what you think about Jesus coming back to life.

20

What does God look like?

You have just heard part of the story of Moses. Perhaps you have heard or read it before. We'll read it again in two parts.

Part 1
Read **Exodus 3:1–6.** (Your leader will help you find Exodus. It is the second book of the Bible.) What colours do you think you would have seen if you'd been there? What else would you have noticed? Can you remember why Moses was looking after sheep in the desert? What had happened when Moses lived in Egypt?

_____

_____

Verse 2 gives a clue about what God looked like to Moses.

The angel of the Lord looked like a f_____ coming from a b_____.

1

My Why Book!

...for children who want answers about God!

Scripture
union
light to live by

207–209 Queensway,
Bletchley,
Milton Keynes
MK2 2EB, UK
www.scriptureunion.org.uk

Name_____

Date_____

Hard issues christians face

The second half of **So, Why God?** helps children answer some of the hard questions that arise when they are trying to live as Christians in God's world and make sense of what is happening all around them. If you are running Part 2 without having done Part 1 with the children, please refer to the notes that precede Part 1 about how **So, Why God?** works.

Why do children ask the questions in Part 2?

Children have a natural desire to know about God, but it often seems that believing in him raises all sorts of other questions. Some will come from their friends who don't believe, some arise as part of school work, others because of a disaster in the news or a family problem. It's often helpful to ask the children where a question comes from.

Why me? in Part 2
Option one: Craft

These take a bit of preparation for each session. Often a ready-made example helps the children to see how to make it. Use the group as an opportunity to talk and build relationships which matter, don't get too distracted with complicated craft work. There isn't much time in the programme anyway.

Option two: Snapshots

In Why6, it was suggested that all the children were given *Snapshots through Mark*, an introductory version of Scripture Union's regular Bible guide for 8- to 11-year-olds. If they have done this and found it helpful, one option in Part 2 is to encourage them to go on reading the Bible with *Snapshots* in the Why me? section. You could get the children to bring their copies of *Snapshots through Mark* and select stories from there to encourage them to continue doing the booklets themselves at home. If they have already done all of this booklet, get them the regular quarterly *Snapshots* and do those with them. After all, what we really want for these children is that they learn how to find their own answers from the Bible. So they need to learn how to read the Bible for themselves.

Experience suggests that very few children manage to do Bible reading notes without some adult encouragement. To include reading *Snapshots* together in each **So, Why God?** session is a really good way to encourage this. You will have to be flexible about how you do this, as some children will race ahead and do a page a day: others will hardly do one in between your sessions.

We did this

After a camp, when we gave *Snapshots* to all the campers, one mum told me that her son had nearly finished his booklet in a few days. The dated *Snapshots* was supposed to last three months! She was especially amazed as he hadn't even wanted to go to church before camp. Something had happened to him there, and his response was to want to get into the Bible.

Option three: What do you think?

As the children have the chance to carry on with *Snapshots* or *Snapshots through Mark* started in Why6, the photocopiable sheets change in style for the second half of **So, Why God?** from word/logic based to a more reflective format. The questions in this section follow on from the main question of the session and give children an opportunity to think about what their answers would be. There are also further questions which children often ask, linking to the main question, with Bible verses which should help to answer them. The children in the group choose one of these questions, read the Bible verses together (or the group leader may read the verse to the children), then they write or draw their answer. The end result should be a set of pages reminding them of what they have done during **So, Why God?** 'What do you think?' makes up to *Snapshots* size, to help the children move on to the dated *Snapshots* afterwards. (You could offer these to the children on the course to encourage them in Bible reading.)

Why7

Luke 14:15–24;
Luke 16:19–31;
Revelation 21:3,4

Aims **To help children realise that anyone can be forgiven for the wrong they have done, and so be invited to go to heaven, thanks to what Jesus did on the cross.**
To help children understand that we have to say yes to Jesus to take up this invitation to heaven.

Do good people go to heaven and bad people go to hell?

What's it all about?

Dispelling misconceptions about heaven and hell.

It is widely held that Christianity teaches that to get to heaven you need to be good, and if you are not you will go to hell. Some people even joke about wanting to go to hell as that's where all their friends will be! This shows a total misunderstanding about the nature of heaven and hell.

So, what is heaven like?

Heaven is a wonderful place with no pain, no death, no crying or grief. God will live with his people there for ever (Revelation 21:3,4). But we need to receive God's invitation, that through Jesus' death and resurrection we are made holy and acceptable to God. Those who don't are eternally separated from God.

What sort of leaders does Why7 need?

We can be sure that we are going to heaven, but we must be humble and honest that it is only because Jesus has forgiven us and is making us to be more like him. We must avoid ever giving the impression that we are good enough by ourselves.

Leaders need to be sensitive to answer awkward questions in thoughtful ways. We must tell the truth as we understand it from the Bible, but make sure it is from the Bible, as there is a lot of folklore on this subject. We need to make sure we share the truth, but we need to say it in ways that encourage faith. In short, as always, we need to let God speak through us. What would Jesus have said?

Whys advice

All sorts of related issues could come up in this session. If there has been a tragedy in the news recently and lots of people, perhaps including children, have died, the children in your group will want to know where they have gone: heaven or hell. Some may want to know about what happens to a baby if it dies. Others might want to know what happens to someone who doesn't even know anything about Jesus when they die. Leaders need to think how they could answer these sorts of questions.

Further reading for leaders:
The Great Divorce, CS Lewis , (Fount, 2002) is very helpful on heaven and hell.

So, why does this question matter?

Death is the ultimate statistic. One in one dies. Everyone asks the question, 'What next?' at some time in their lives. It matters, because what we believe affects our lives here and now. Paul said, 'If our hope in Christ is good only for this life, we are worse off than anyone else' (1 Corinthians 15:19).

To Jesus, dying is just like going to sleep. How else can we explain his words to Jairus in Luke 8:52, and to his disciples in John 11:11? Death is not something to be feared by the Christian: Jesus has defeated death.

7

So, why do children ask, 'Do good people go to heaven and bad people go to hell?'

Most children seem to presume that people they love who die will have gone to heaven. Well-meaning adults have told them this. Of course it is a comfort for them to think that Gran is in a wonderful place, happy with Jesus. So this session could be difficult for some children, especially if they realise that their Gran didn't ever show any signs of asking Jesus to forgive her.

Throughout home and school life adults reward children for doing good things. This is often part of training a child to do right and to learn how to behave. It can lead to a reward culture, which naturally leads to a similar belief about what happens after death.

Church children

'I went to my grandad's funeral and they put him in the ground.' This can be difficult for a child to understand. We tell the child that Grandad has gone to be with Jesus, but they see the coffin containing the body put into the ground. This is a good time to explain that the body in the coffin is only the body now. What made it really Grandad was his spirit that lived in the body.

Why in

Make sure you are ready with this activity for the children to do as soon as they arrive. Choose one of the following activities:

①1 For me heaven would be?
(10 minutes)

You will need:
- paper
- pencils, crayons or felt-tip pens, rubber, sharpener

Everyone draws a multi-picture (that is, lots of little pictures on one sheet) of all the things that would make a place heaven for them. It will be helpful if the group leader has one they did earlier to show what is needed. This is not meant to be too serious, so having pictures of chocolate, a swimming pool or a computer game is fine. You may prefer not to include people in your drawing for now to allow children to decide for themselves what they would like. Give the children time to complete their drawings, but try to have a couple of minutes for them to explain them to the rest of the group. If

necessary, stop them part way through drawing to chat and let them finish their pictures later.

①2 Review from Why4
(10 minutes)

Do the 'Make the punishment fit' activity from Why4 (page 34). Briefly remind the children when you last did this activity and what Jesus has done. Bring out the wood and nails from the 'What now?' activity from page 36. Let the children hold the items and think again about why Jesus died and what that means. This will lead into saying how Jesus' actions open the way to heaven, if we accept what he has done because he has made us holy.

If you did neither of these activities before, you could still use the nails and wood to help children remember what Jesus has done for them. Chat a bit about what the children think. Link in to what you are going to be talking about in this session.

So, Why God?

①1 What does the Bible say?
(5 minutes)

Memory verse John 6:37
This verse is aimed at helping children to realise that through Jesus' actions, God will accept us all. He wants us all to come to him. Get all the children to click their fingers to a rhythm, to the following words that Jesus said (taken from the Good News Bible). Those who can't click their fingers can clap two fingers against their other palm, which makes a similar noise. Say the words in the rhythm, the words in bold being said on the beat:

I will **ne**ver **turn** a**way**
Anyone who **comes** to **me**
John six verse **thir**ty-**sev'n**

To help the children learn the words, have them written on a white board and wipe out a word or two each time you say the verse. Or write the verse on a large sheet of paper. Then, after you say the verse, fold the paper twice, and tear a piece out. When you open it up, there will be a hole somewhere in the verse. Keep removing bits of the verse, saying it each time, until there is nothing left. Then see who can still say it by themselves.

7

⊕2 What's the story?
(10 minutes)

**The parable of the wedding feast
(Luke 14:15–21)**

BEGINNING
'Now is the time!' 'Everything is ready!' 'Tell them all to come!'

Explain that going to parties or to a wedding was a bit different in Jesus' day. You didn't get an invitation with a time and date on it which you had to reply to. You were told there would be a party, and then someone was sent to get you when everything was ready.

Jesus told a story about a man who was planning a party. He had told all the people that it would be happening and he set about getting everything ready. When he had finally arranged all the food, drink and the entertainment, he sent out one of his servants to tell everyone he had invited that the party was about to start! He was very excited!

MAIN POINT
But when the servant got to each guest's house, every guest had an excuse not to come. 'Oh, I've just bought a big field and I'm going to have a look at it.' 'Well, I've just got some new oxen and I want to see how well they work!' 'I've just got married, so I can't come!'

Can you believe it? Nobody wanted to come. The man was really upset! Ask the children how they would feel if all their friends said they didn't want to come to their party.

ENDING
So what did the man do? Did he sit around, lonely and miserable because none of the people he had invited came to his party? No! He went out and invited more people so that his house would be full for the party! Full of people who had accepted his invitation.

Whys advice
Telling a story well is a dying art. It is not hard to learn, but needs practice. It is much better to tell a story than to read one, although children do like having stories read to them.

To tell a story you must know the story well. For a Bible story, read it in different versions of the Bible. Especially try to read it in Bibles that are better for children, like the *Good News Bible*, the *Contemporary English Version* or the *New International Readers' Version* (a simplified NIV). Then work out three things for your story: a good beginning, the main point and the ending.

⊕3 What's the answer?
(5 minutes)

Have an invitation to heaven (see page 21) to show the children. Say that God wants us to be his friend, but to be his friend we have to say sorry for all the things we have done wrong. When we say sorry for all the wrong things we have done (like the prayer on page 17), and say thank you to Jesus for taking all the punishment, then we accept God's invitation to heaven.

Say that nothing we do can get us into heaven. Doing good things is not enough. None of the people in the story who were invited from the streets and alleys in the town were 'good' people. They weren't the richest, the most popular or the most powerful. They were the poor, the beggars and the disabled (verse 21). Being the best isn't what matters. It is accepting God's invitation to heaven; it's saying 'yes' to Jesus that counts.

And what will heaven be like? Read Revelation 21:3,4 and ask the children what heaven will be like. Ask them to think about what makes them cry, or causes pain. God says that there won't be any crying or pain in heaven. If we accept God's invitation to heaven then, when we get there, all those things will be wiped away.

Remind the children again of why Jesus died. He died so that we could be forgiven for the times we hurt people. Then God can start to change us to be more like Jesus.

Perhaps some children will never have thought about this before, and we need to give them a chance to respond to God about it. Be sensitive to this possibility. Have a prayer card ready to offer to any children who might be thinking about it. For more advice on this, please see the section 'Helping Children Respond' on page 10.

Why me?

🕐1 What can I do?
(20 minutes)

The group time is an important opportunity to talk in smaller groups about what children are thinking and to encourage further questions. The options are craft, *Snapshots* or the **What do you think?** pages.

Craft: An invitation to heaven

The idea is to pretend you are God or Jesus, and make an invitation that God might give to his people to come to heaven. It would be helpful to read John 14:1,2 before you start.

You will need:

- A5 card, enough for one sheet each
- art materials, appropriate to your group and setting
- a finished card to show the children what sort of thing to do

Photocopy the invitation on page 21 and give one to each child for them to decorate with words or pictures that show what heaven is like. For example, draw some tears, and then big bold black lines to cross them out; the same with a picture showing pain, and death. Encourage the children to use their imagination, and draw other things they know about heaven. They could add in some of the phrases from John 14:1,2. Ask the children if anyone knows what RSVP stands for, and be sure to talk about how you could reply to God.

Be sensitive about the way you talk about heaven. Children may get so excited about being invited to 'the best party ever' that they want to go there straight away! Explain that God wants us to enjoy life on earth and has lots of plans for us but he also has a place in heaven prepared for those who accept his invitation.

Snapshots

Use *Snapshots through Mark* or the regular dated *Snapshots* with the children in their groups, to help them learn how to read the Bible for themselves. Day 13 in *Snapshots through Mark* is the story of Jesus becoming 'whiter than white' on top of the mountain. Perhaps this gives a little glimpse of what Jesus will be like in heaven.

What do you think?

This is the final group option. You will need pencils or pens, and crayons or felt-tip pens if the children would like to draw their answers. Turn to number one and ask the children to write down what they would say to answer the question of the day, if someone asked it now. You may have to help them work out what they want to put, but try not to give them your answer again. Let them write or draw it in their own way.

On the next page are some extra questions that link to the main question. Let the children agree which question to do and try to answer it in the rest of the group time. Alongside each question are some Bible verses to read, which should help. After some chatting get them to write or draw their answers in the booklet.

🕐2 What now?
(5 minutes)

Ask the children to sit down and hold their invitations to heaven in their hands if they have made them. Remind them that God invites everyone to come to him. For a few moments there will be quiet while each child thinks about how they want to respond to God's invitation.

Then pray this prayer:

Thank you God that you want everyone to come to you. Thank you that it's like being invited to one big party. Help each one of us to accept your invitation when we feel ready.

Postbox

Explain to the children that you are offering to answer other questions, or maybe put a leader 'On the spot'. If they want to ask questions about God, Jesus or the Bible, get them to write them down and put them in the Postbox. Be sure to use what they write next time you meet.

7

Why8

Luke 7:36–50

Aims **To explore how we know that God is really there and that he really loves us.**

How do you know you are right about God?

What's it all about?

The question for this session is one that children often ask in circle time at school. Underlying it is the more subjective question:

'How do you know that God loves you?'
This is the more important personal question, but it is rarely asked in a group, so the headline question may be easier to handle. Another commonly asked question related to this is: 'How do you know God hears when you pray?' This is addressed in Why10.

What sort of leaders does Why8 need?

Leaders tackling this question with children need a mixture of assurance of their own faith and sympathy for those who find it hard to believe. Thinking back over the way God has led us to trust him will help build up our faith.

Leaders need to be careful that their own strong assurance of God doesn't put off children who don't have it. Some children find it really hard to be sure that God is real, especially as they can't see him. These children don't need leaders who are dogmatic and say that it's obvious God exists! They need someone who will listen to their doubts and worries. Someone who will hear the underlying concerns like, 'Even if there is a God, he wouldn't be interested in me.'

So, why does this question matter?

Everything in our faith depends on God actually being there, that he really exists and is like the Bible says he is.

HOW DO YOU KNOW HE IS THERE?
Even though we can't see God we can see the effect God has on our world. We may not be able to prove conclusively that God is there, but we can give some reasons why we believe he is there:

- Creation. Looking at the beauty around us helps us believe that there is someone great behind it all.
- When we see a real change in someone's life after they start to believe in God.

- When we pray, sometimes, not always, we see God acting in amazing ways. We must be honest in what we say about answers to prayer, if we are to help children truly believe in God. Some people make it sound as if everything they ever ask God for happens immediately.

DOES GOD REALLY LOVE ME?
This question is often the real one at the heart of the others. So many people can't believe that, if there is a God, he could be interested in them, let alone actually love them as they are. The truth is that God cannot love us any more than he does now, no matter what we might do or say. He cannot love us any less either. God is love.

So, why do children ask, 'How do you know you are right about God?'

Sorting out fact and fantasy

As children grow up they begin to sort out which things are really true and which are make-believe. Much of this is worked out from 7 to 11 years. This is when children usually learn the truth about Father Christmas, the tooth fairy and others.

Insecurity

Many children grow up not quite sure in lots of ways. Some are not sure how they should behave, as sometimes they can do what they like, but other times they are told off severely for trivial things. If they are not sure about so much in their lives, it is crucial to them to know whether they can be sure of God or not.

Low self-esteem

Lots of children have difficulty believing anyone really likes them. Perhaps this applies to many adults as well. It's often not rational, but it affects us all the same. We think that we are no good, we have no real abilities and everyone else has more brains than us. This is not how God sees us, but many of us find it hard to believe that God really accepts us as we are.

What about other gods?

Children often ask about 'other gods' so we must be ready for this. One helpful way is to recognise that the Bible says that only the LORD God is real. The first commandment tells us to 'Worship no god but me' (Exodus 20:3). The second commandment tells us not to worship idols. There are, however, lots of passages about how we should treat people who worship different gods. (The phrase 'people of other faiths' doesn't appear in the Bible. Instead it refers to aliens or foreigners who would have worshipped gods other than Yahweh.) Nearly all of these passages instruct God's people not to oppress others (Exodus 23:9; Zechariah 7:10), but to mirror God's love for people of other faiths (Deuteronomy 10:18,19). Jesus showed love and acceptance to the Samaritan woman at the well (John 4:1–41) and tells us to love our neighbours (Mark 12:31).

So we have to help children hold these two things together. We worship the one true God and love those who worship other gods in other ways. For more information, go to www.faithtofaith.org.uk

Church children

Church children have grown up being told about God. They often know lots about him, but many come to a time in their lives when they have to work out whether they will believe God is real for themselves. For some this is a normal step on the way to real, personal faith, a step known as searching for faith. Going through this phase can be tough for the parents and friends of the child, but leads to a stronger, more thought-out faith at the other side.

Why in

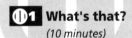

⏸1 What's that?
(10 minutes)

For this you need a variety of games where the children have to guess what something is, without seeing it. It may be best to have them set out so that children come as a group to a game, rather than setting up individual ones for each group. Here are some suggestions; you may be able to think of others:

- **Feely bag** – A shopping bag (not a thin carrier bag) with about five or six items in it, to be guessed by feeling only. Once they have had a feel, they must write down or draw the items.
- **Smelly vision** – This is a tray of bowls with different scents in each. Try to get things that can't be guessed by what they look like. For example: antiseptic liquid, perfume, spirit

vinegar (clear sort), flavoured water, peppermint or almond flavouring.
- **Sounds like** – A tape of sound effects to listen to and guess. The BBC do an excellent sound effects CD, but you can just record some local sounds, like a door closing, car starting, mobile phone ringing, computer connecting to the internet, microwave cooking, washing machine spinning.

After each game, check how many each person got right, and see if one is better at feeling, whilst another is better at hearing. Ask the children which game was the easiest and why. Talk about how we know things are really there.

So, Why God?

⊕1 On the spot
(5 minutes)

This is a chance for the children to hear personal answers from one of the leaders. It is a powerful thing to do, when someone talks about what they believe. To help leaders who are worried about this, prepare some questions in advance. If the children have put questions in the Postbox, use them if the leader is willing.

Here are some questions that relate to this session to get you started:
- When did you first hear about God?
- What helps you to be sure about God?
- If someone isn't sure God loves them, what would you say to help them?

⊕2 What does the Bible say?
(5 minutes)

People can doubt the Bible: that was our question for Why6, so refer to that if you need to. For this session we will continue to use Bible stories, with other material, to help children believe that God is real.

⊕3 What's the Story?
(15 minutes)

At Simon the Pharisee's house, (Luke 7:36–50)
Another way to look at a story you are going to tell is to think of it as a problem and a solution to that problem. These are set out here, including a main point that you might like to weave into the story as you tell it. Copy the pictures on page 19 onto card and use them to tell the story in your own words. If you did the

8

'smelly vision' Why in activity, use the perfume in your telling of the story.

THE PROBLEM FOR THIS STORY

The problem in this story is the woman who lived a sinful life (people always worry about what to say if the children ask what she had done, but they rarely do – if they do, tell them to look in the Bible – it doesn't say!). Did she wonder if the stories about Jesus were true? Did she feel that Jesus couldn't possibly love her? Did she really expect what happened? There is a second problem, which is that Simon couldn't accept the way Jesus responded to her.

THE MAIN POINT

The main point of the story is that Jesus forgave the woman all her wrong. She showed her love for him by her behaviour. We might say that this showed how sorry she was about the life she led. Simon couldn't imagine any prophet from God allowing such a woman to touch him.

THE SOLUTION TO THE PROBLEM

The woman had her sin forgiven by Jesus. He showed that he loved her. Others there found this hard to comprehend. The Bible makes it clear that the woman was forgiven and she was right about Jesus. He did love her, and he would forgive her. He will do the same for us.

If you want an alternative way of presenting this story, it is told on the *Streetwise DVD*, episode 3, 'The Rich House' (SU, 1 84427 111 0).

4 What's the answer?
(5 minutes)

The Bible makes it very clear that God is really there. The children may object if you give them a chance, saying that you would expect the Bible to say that. To anticipate this, tell the children that you know some people aren't sure about the Bible, but there are other reasons that you believe in God. Here are three more:

• Because of the wonderful world around us. It is easier to believe that God made it all (especially its beauty) than that it happened by chance.
• Because of the difference we see in people who believe in God, especially when the change is quite pronounced.
• Because we have seen God answering our prayers. When we pray, sometimes, not always, we see God giving amazing answers that just couldn't have happened by chance.

Why me?

1 What can I do?
(20 minutes)

Make the most of the opportunity together as you work on one of the options: Craft or Snapshots or **What do you think?** pages. Use the time to talk more about this session's question and related questions that the children may have.

The Craft: 'The JESUS is God' chart

You will need:
• large sheet of paper
• large sheet of card
• small sheets of paper
• thick marker pen
• felt-tip pens and colouring pencils
• scissors
• ribbon

With the children, think of things that help us to believe that JESUS is God. List them in different headings on the large sheet of paper so everyone can see. Headings could include:
• Seeing
• Hearing
• Touching
• Knowing
• Reading
• Feeling inside

Get a volunteer to write 'JESUS is God' in the middle of the large sheet of card. Then share out all the things you thought of, perhaps by giving each list to a couple of children. They then draw the items and the heading, and cut them out. Glue them in a group on the large card, with a ribbon from the items to the phrase 'JESUS is God'. The group will have then made a chart to help them think about how they can be more certain that God is real.

Snapshots

Use *Snapshots through Mark* or the regular dated *Snapshots* with the children in their groups, to help them learn how to read the Bible for themselves. Day 11 in *Snapshots through Mark* is the story of Jesus asking his disciples who they thought he was. This could be a helpful way to continue the discussions about being right about Jesus.

What do you think? pages

This is the final group option. You will need pencils or pens, and crayons or felt-tips if the children would like to draw their answers. Turn to number two, and ask the children to write down what they would say to answer the question of the day, if someone asked it now. You may have to help them work out what they want to put, but try not just to give them your answer again, but let them write or draw it in their own way.

On the next page are some extra questions that link to the main question. Let the children agree on one question to try and answer during the rest of the group time. Alongside each question are some Bible verses to read, which should help. After some chatting get them to write or draw their answers in the booklet.

02 What now?
(5 minutes)

At the end of the group time, take a minute or two to pray. Prayers could include saying sorry for doing wrong things. They may want to ask Jesus to forgive them as he did the woman in the story. Others may want to talk to God about their doubts and ask him to help them believe more strongly.

Postbox

Remind the children that they can write questions about God, Jesus or the Bible to the leaders and put them in the Postbox. If there are other things they want to write about, they can put those in as well. Remind them that a leader will be 'On the spot' soon.

So, Who is God? **link**
Question 3 (page 16) may be helpful in looking at this topic, as would Question 13 (page 52).

Why9

John 20:24–29;
Acts 2:1–11

Aim **To talk about what God is like, including that he is holy and that he is spirit. To think especially about God the Holy Spirit.**

Why can't you see God?

What's it all about?

Children often say they have difficulty believing in God as they can't see him. This reflects their concrete way of thinking and seeing the world. Here we look at two reasons why we can't see God:

- God is so holy that people can't look at him and survive.
- God is spirit and is not naturally visible to our physical eyes.

What sort of leaders does Why9 need?

Those who know God. This may sound obvious, but it is easy to rush into answering children's questions about God based on what we have read, or even merely the material in this book. As leaders we need to make sure we are in touch with God ourselves. We must take time to renew our relationship with God. How can we introduce children to God if we are passing strangers with him ourselves? Let us take seriously our call from God, as Jesus called his disciples to 'be with him' (Mark 3:14).

Whys advice

We need leaders who are able to listen. Really listen. Listen without always thinking about what they need to say next. Listen to that which is behind what they are being told. Listen to God, who will lead us and give us the right way to lead others to him, if we are open to him ourselves.

Understand children

Leaders need to be on the same wavelength as children. That is, to realise what sort of things they can or can't understand and how spiritual they can be. They have had less time to grow cynical by the pressures of the world. Yet children have difficulty with long words; with unfamiliar concepts; sometimes with abstract ideas; or with things that are completely outside their experience.

Whys advice

It's not hard to discover whether children can understand what we are talking about. If we make sure we are in conversation with them, rather than talking at them all the time, we will soon find out what they understand. Asking the children questions is always a good way. Getting them to answer other children's questions is also helpful.

Don't have all the answers

It is fine to say to the children that you don't know. Some of their questions don't have any easy answers. If you genuinely don't know, offer to find out. Sometimes it is helpful to let others have a go at answering a question before you, or instead of you. Children may not get it completely right (they may even be wrong, which needs careful handling), but you will learn more about the child who answers, if you let them try.

So, why does this question matter?
The physical and the spiritual

We often think that the most real things in our lives are those that we can see and touch. This is the physical world that we are naturally equipped to be part of. As we get to know God we realise that there is a whole other world out there – the spiritual world. We are also equipped to be part of this spiritual world, but it is often more difficult for us to understand.

So, why do children ask, 'Why can't you see God?'

Children are taught in science at school to watch and see what happens. Experiments are carefully set up to show how materials behave. Observation and proof are key ideas, so how might children react when they can't observe or prove God? Perhaps having a blind person to visit the group for this question would put a whole new slant on the session, helping the children to realise that belief need not be based on sight.

Television is a big factor in the lives of many children. They absorb so much information through their eyes via that screen or the computer.

It's not unusual for children to have invisible friends. One child insisted on another place being laid at the table for every meal, especially if it was something he liked to eat! Other children play for hours with their imaginary friend. As they grow older most children grow out of these things, so they have to work out what to do about God, who wants to be their friend (so they are told) but who is invisible. Why would he make himself invisible? they might think.

Why in

◗1 Invisble Quick draw
(10 minutes)

Give out refreshments as children arrive, if this is appropriate.

You will need:
- 'invisible quick-draw' cards (see below)
- paper
- pencil
- egg timer or stopwatch (optional)

Prepare a set of small cards with the name of something invisible on each one. Take it in turns around your group to draw something that will help the rest of the group to guess what it is. Usual rules of games like this apply:
- No words or letters can be drawn.
- No talking by the person drawing, except to say yes or no to a guess.

To add excitement use an egg timer and gain a point if the group can guess what you draw in the time it takes for the sand to trickle through, or use a stopwatch.

You will need enough cards for everyone in your group to have at least two turns. Here are some ideas of words you could put on your 'invisible quick-draw' cards: wind, air, radio waves, sound, atoms, love, strength, God (make this the last one).

So, Why God?

◗1 What do you know?
(5 minutes)

Ask everyone to think about one thing they know about God (apart from the fact that you can't see him, that's too easy). Give them a minute to think, and then go round the whole group and write on flip chart paper or a large sheet of card what they say about God. To start off with, write down 'God?' and then 'You can't see him'. It doesn't matter if two people say the same thing, write it down anyway.

Talk briefly about what is written on the sheet. Ask them if they want to say anything about something someone else said. See if most of the comments are really about God the Father or about Jesus. Seeing as most children know less about the Holy Spirit, it is likely that there will be few comments about him. If all the comments are about God the Father, explain this, before you move on.

Do the same with Jesus. Ask them to think of something about Jesus. Try to avoid just saying the same as we said about God the Father. If all is going well, try writing up, 'The Holy Spirit' and see what the children know about him already.

◗2 What does the Bible say?
(5 minutes)

Acts 2:1–11
This is the story of the Holy Spirit coming to fill all of the believers. Checking Acts 1:15 with Acts 2:1, it would seem that about 120 were filled with the Holy Spirit initially. Until this time the believers had met privately, perhaps not daring to speak in public, perhaps remembering what Jesus said about waiting for the Holy Spirit to come. In any case, the coming of the Holy Spirit had a dramatic impact on them all, and thrust them out among the people who were gathered in Jerusalem for the feast of Pentecost (the old Jewish festival of the first harvest).

9

◉3 What's the story?
(15 minutes)

Remember that to tell a good story you need to have a good beginning, a clear main point and know how to end. Here are some ideas on telling this story but put them into your own words, using the pictures on page 20 as indicated:

BEGINNING
We were all together, about 120 of us in the one room. It was pretty full. *(Show picture 1.)* One minute everything was quiet, then the next there was a loud noise like the wind, only nothing was getting blown around. We all looked around wondering what was happening, but we couldn't see anything to start off with. Then, starting with one or two, we saw little flames spreading around the room. Not like anything was actually burning, but they just touched everyone there. *(Ask the children to draw flames on to picture 1.)* Wow! People started to talk to each other, but not just in their own language, in all different ones. The noise of talking grew louder and louder and louder...

MAIN POINT
God has come down and filled each one of us with his Holy Spirit. Apart from a little flame touching us, we couldn't see anything or anyone, but it had an amazing effect on us all. We started to do things we would never have done before. Before the fire came we were scared, and I don't think any of us could speak in those other languages either. *(Show picture 2.)* But soon we were all outside, telling other people about God...

ENDING
We couldn't see God, but we certainly knew he had come to us. Jesus told us he would send the Holy Spirit and he did. Peter was able to tell a whole crowd of people about Jesus. *(Show picture 3.)* It was all because of the power of the Holy Spirit!

◉4 What's the answer?
(5 minutes)

Chat with the children to help them think about the answer to the question. Consider two basic answers (as detailed below). The first is what we have been talking about in the story, so major on that. Only add the second answer if they have got the first, and there is time.

GOD IS SPIRIT
We can't see God because he is basically made of different stuff to us. We are made of flesh, bones, blood and lots of other things that are all physical. We can see most physical things, except the things in our game at the start of this session. God isn't made of physical things. When Jesus came, he was God taking on physical form, and then people could see God. But God is spirit, and our physical eyes can't see spiritual things. When the Holy Spirit came, he made himself look like a flame, but then people couldn't see him when he had gone into them. Notice that he went into lots of people, and when they started to go out talking to other people, he was still in them. This shows he can be in all of us who believe, at the same time.

There is something good about this. When Jesus was here on earth, he only stayed in one place at a time, like we do. This meant that only people in Israel saw him. Now Jesus has gone back to heaven, he has sent the Holy Spirit, who is still God like Jesus, but he is spirit. This means he can be everywhere at the same time. So he can be with us in this country, helping us, and at the same time, he can be with Christians in Africa or America. If he still had a physical body like Jesus had when he was on earth, he wouldn't be with everyone who believes in him at the same time.

GOD IS HOLY
Another reason that we can't see God is that he doesn't let us see him. In the Bible, God told Moses that 'I won't let you see my face, because anyone who sees my face will die' (Exodus 33:20). This is because God is holy. Holy means very special, so special in fact that just to look at God would kill us. One way God is special is that he is completely good and pure. We do things wrong, so to look at such a pure and good God would kill us. It's not that God would kill us on purpose, if we saw him, but it would just happen because of what he is like.

Why me?

◉1 What can I do?
(20 minutes)

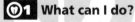

Now is the time to go back into groups. Use this time to chat about the question, and the answers. See if you can discover how much the children understand. There are three options: a craft, *Snapshots* or the **What do you think?** pages.

Craft: A fire poster

You will need:

- sheets of tissue paper in fire colours, ie yellow, orange, red, brown
- pencils and felt-tip pens
- scissors
- glue
- a large sheet of paper or card per group or, to make a really big fire, just one giant sheet for everyone

Before the session, prepare a few flame templates cut out of stiff cardboard, so that children can just draw round the shape onto the tissue paper. Have various flame shapes. Some children may like to draw their own shape. Each child can do several flames on different coloured paper. Cut out the shapes. When you have lots, stick them onto the large sheet of card to make the fire. Someone should oversee this, so that the fire is put together well. As you do this, talk to the children about what they thought of the story, what questions they still have or what they have learnt.

The first to put their flames on the card can start to cut out some letters to stick across the top of the poster: The Holy Spirit Came.

Snapshots

Use *Snapshots through Mark* or the regular dated *Snapshots* with the children in their groups, to help them learn how to read the Bible for themselves. If you are using *Snapshots through Mark*, Day 8 is about seeing Jesus.

What do you think?

This is the final group option. You will need pencils or pens, and crayons or felt-tip pens if the children would like to draw their answers.

Turn to number three, and ask the children to write down what they would say to answer the question of the day, if someone asked it now. You may have to help them work out what they want to put, but try not just to give them your answer again, but let them write or draw it in their own way. (You will learn a lot about how much they have understood about the discussion you had earlier! You may also discover a child's perspective on the answer which will help you with future questions.)

Underneath and on the next page are some extra questions that link to the main question. Let the children agree on one question to try and answer in the rest of the group time. Alongside each question are some Bible verses to read, which should help. After some chatting get them to write or draw their answers in the booklet.

⏱2 What now?
(5 minutes)

Give each child a few Post-it notes and a pencil. Ask the children to think about any prayers they would like to pray. These could include thanking God that he is with us, even though we can't see him, or asking him to help us with any difficult things we have to do. If you did the flame poster craft, stick the Post-it notes around the poster, or stick them on a wall for everyone to pray. Spend a few moments, praying some of the prayers on the Post-it notes.

Postbox

Remind the children that they can write questions about God, Jesus or the Bible to the leaders and put them in the Postbox. If there are other things they want to write about, they can put those in as well. Remind them that a leader will be 'On the spot' soon.

Aims **To help children
realise that God wants us
to pray.**
**To help children believe
that God hears them when
they pray.**

How do you know God hears you when you pray?

What's it all about?

WHAT IS PRAYER?
Prayer is something that all Christians know
about, but few of us make the most of. When
you think about it, prayer is the most amazing
thing ever – mere mortals communicating with
the God who made the whole universe! This very
fact can make us think that God wouldn't be
interested in our little lives.

HOW DO WE KNOW GOD HAS ANSWERED?
Being sure that God hears our prayers isn't
simple. Sometimes we pray and God does what
we ask for, which is great. But other times, we
pray and it seems as if nothing happens. Then it
is hard to believe that God has heard our prayer
– how do we know? As with many things in the
Christian life we must accept it by faith, based on
what we know about God and what he says in
the Bible.

What sort of leaders does Why10 need?

As with so many of these hard questions that
Christians face, this subject needs leaders who
are honest and open, and willing to admit that
they don't actually know everything. It doesn't
help a child who doubts that God hears their
prayer if a leader is bursting with confidence and
absolutely certain about prayer.

On the other hand, we do need to encourage
children to pray and to believe what God
promises. Leaders should share their experiences
of praying, both when God clearly does what
they have asked and when he doesn't. Children
need to see that prayer is more about our
relationship with God, than it is about getting
what we want.

So, why does this question matter?

Prayer is a major part of the Christian life.
Although many Christians would be embarrassed
if you asked them about their prayer life, Jesus
told us clearly that we should pray. He taught his
disciples how to pray (Matthew 6), and
demonstrated in his own life the importance he
placed on prayer, often by spending hours alone
with God. In the same way, we as his disciples
need to value spending time with God in prayer.
We invite children to become friends with Jesus.
It is a strange friendship if that doesn't include
talking and listening. In fact, the friendship will
very likely fade away without this. He wants us
to talk to him, he wants to communicate with us
and show us the way in our lives. This is so often
done as we pray with him. Being sure that God
hears us when we pray makes our whole
relationship with God more alive and immediate.
If our prayers seem to bounce off the ceiling, we
often feel remote and out of touch with God.

Further reading for leaders:
Too busy not to pray Bill Hybels (IVP)
Don't just stand there… Pray something Ron
Dunn (Zondervan)
How to pray when life hurts Roy Lawrence (SU)

So, why do children ask, 'How do you know God hears you when you pray?'

We know a friend has heard us by their response.
Many a child will want you to look straight at
them when they talk to you, to make sure you
are listening to them. We can't see God, so it is
harder to be sure that he is listening to us.

The fact that God doesn't always do what we
ask him compounds this for children, whose

thinking is very black and white. They may pray that their sick rabbit won't die – surely God would want to grant that – but the rabbit dies. They may pray that hungry children in Africa get enough food – God can do that, and surely loves the children enough, but it doesn't happen.

Many children become used to adults not listening to them, especially those who are important. Other adults sometimes excuse these sorts of people by explaining to children how busy they are. God is the most important person in the whole universe, so children can easily think that he is too busy, that he is not interested in them.

Church children

Church children will be used to praying in church, but may find some prayers in church too long or the language too difficult. They may wonder if God will only really hear you if you pray like some adults do. Other church children will be used to praying and will love to pray in our small groups. Their prayers are often refreshingly simple and trusting. They can encourage others in our groups to want to pray also.

Why in

Make sure you are ready for the children to start this activity as soon as they arrive. Choose one of the following:

◀1 Chinese whispers
(10 minutes)

With your group in a circle, whisper something to the child sitting next to you, they have to whisper to the next child, and so on. The last one tells you what they heard. See if it is the same as your original sentence. Each time, the leader should move round one place, so a different child starts and ends. Prepare a series of phrases, getting harder to hear. These will get you started:

I hope you can hear this all right.
There's something funny going on here.
I wonder what this message will end up sounding like with all this whispering.
Do you think that the message is getting through to everyone in this group?

◀2 Charades
(10 minutes)

Think up a list of TV programmes, films and books for children. Get the group to divide into two teams with team members sitting together. Ask for a volunteer to come up and mime the first title for the rest of their group to guess the answer. Continue the game by giving the next title to a child in the opposite team and finish once everyone has had a go at miming. Score points each time the team guesses the answer correctly. You may want to set a time limit on each title to keep the game moving.

So, Why God?

◀1 What does the Bible say?
(5 minutes)

Memory verse John 14:13
'Ask me, and I will do whatever you ask. This way, the Son will bring honour to the Father.'

Print out the words of this verse in large letters onto several sheets of A4 paper, two or three words per sheet. Hand out the sheets of paper to the children as they are sitting, in the order of the verse so that everyone can read the verse correctly. Say the verse through then ask them to choose a paper to get rid of. Say the verse again. Repeat until there are no sheets of paper left and you are all still saying the verse. See if anyone will dare to say it on their own.

◀2 What's the story?
(15 minutes)

Nehemiah 1:1 – 2:8
Remember that a good story needs a problem, and the story is all about how it is solved. It is fairly obvious what the problem is for Nehemiah. Use pictures from page 65 of *How to cheat at visual aids Old Testament*, (SU) to help you tell the stories.

PROBLEM
Nehemiah was sad. His brother had just arrived from their home town and it was a mess. The walls were broken down and the large wooden gates were burnt and horrible. It was just as if the street where you live had been broken up and made into rubble.

10

THE MAIN POINT
Nehemiah prayed about this, even owning up to God (confessing) lots of things the people of his country had done wrong. Read some parts of verse 6 or 7, and then maybe verse 11 all from chapter 1.

THE SOLUTION
Point out to the children that Nehemiah didn't get an answer for four months (2:1). God had heard his prayer, but Nehemiah had to wait until God did something. It was a surprising and frightening experience for Nehemiah. The king spotted him looking sad (he could probably have had his head cut off for looking sad in the king's presence). Nehemiah was startled, but had to answer. After the next question Nehemiah prayed. The rest of the story is about the answer to his prayer.

⊙3 What's the answer?
(5 minutes)

Ask the children what they think is the answer to the question for this session now they have heard the story. Make sure they agree that God answered Nehemiah's prayer. Quiz them a bit to check they remember how long it took for the answer. Ask them if they think God heard the prayer straight away, or it took a long time for God to hear it. Get them thinking and talking about the different ways God may answer our prayers. How did he answer Nehemiah's prayer?

Whys advice
One helpful way to remember how God answers our prayers is using a traffic light. God always answers our prayers, but sometimes he says no (RED), sometimes he says wait (YELLOW) and sometimes he says yes (GREEN).

Another helpful way of talking about prayer is thinking about talking to someone on the telephone. You can't see them, but still they hear you, and if you listen carefully you can hear them. You may have to talk through with the children how we hear God. You may be surprised at how much they know about this. If you have a mobile phone with a speaker, you could even phone someone to illustrate this (warn them beforehand!)

Why me?

⊙1 What can I do?
(20 minutes)

Now is the time to go back into groups. Use this time to chat about the question, and the answers. See if you can discover how much the children understand. There are three options: craft, *Snapshots* or the **What do you think?** pages.

Craft: A prayer book
You will need:
- A5 paper in various colours (five different colours if possible)
- A5 thin card, one sheet per child
- pencils and felt-tip pens
- a stapler that can reach to the middle of the paper

Get the children to draw round their hand onto the card, so that when the card is folded in half, the fingers and thumb will be on the front. Write on the hand-shape:
- 'thanks' in the thumb
- 'family' in the index finger
- 'teachers and leaders' in the middle finger
- 'sick people' in the fourth finger
- 'me' in the little finger

The children can choose different paper colours for different types of prayers. If you have five colours, then stack one piece of each colour paper together with the card cover, and fold them all in half to make the booklet. Open out and staple, remembering to make sure the hand-shape is on the front cover.

To remind them what each page is for, they can draw round that finger or thumb on the page itself and write the word in it. Then ask them to write one prayer on each page. Encourage them to keep their prayer book and write or draw in it the things they talk to God about. Suggest that they leave space by each prayer to write down an answer when they feel God has given them one.

Whys advice
By now you should know your children well enough to know how much help they will need in writing prayers. You might need to provide sample prayers for them to copy, or they may be fine with a little bit of guidance.

10

Snapshots

Use *Snapshots through Mark* or the regular dated *Snapshots* with the children in their groups, to help them learn how to read the Bible for themselves. If you are using *Snapshots through Mark*, Day 14 shows that Jesus wants children to come to him.

What do you think?

This is the final group option. You will need pencils or pens, and crayons or felt-tip pens if the children would like to draw their answers.

Turn to number four, and ask the children to write down what they would say to answer the question of the day, if someone asked it now. You may have to help them work out what they want to put, but try not just to give them your answer again, but let them write or draw it in their own way. (You will learn a lot about how much they have understood about the discussion you had earlier! You may also discover a child's perspective on the answer which will help you with future questions.)

Underneath and on the next page (of the booklet) are some extra questions that link to the main question. Let the children agree on one question to try and answer during the rest of the group time. Alongside each question are some Bible verses to read, which should help. After some chatting get them to write or draw their answers in the booklet.

 **What now?**
(5 minutes)

At the end of the group time, take a minute or two to pray. Start using your prayer books, if you made them. Prayers could include thanking God that he does hear our prayers, and asking him to help us be patient for his answers. (Write or draw these on the appropriate pages of the book.)

Postbox

Remind the children that they can write questions about God, Jesus or the Bible to the leaders and put them in the Postbox. If there are other things they want to write about, they can put those in as well.

So, Who is God? **link**
This question is also answered in *So Who is God?* as question 14 (page 56).

Why11

John 11:1–44;
(John 9:1–3)

Aims **To help children see that we all contribute to the problem of 'bad things happening'.
To show that God loves us even when bad things happen to us.**

Why does God let bad things happen to good people?

What's it all about?

There are both general and specific questions about suffering that we can consider.

Why do people suffer?

Many adults struggle with the problem of why people suffer, often through no obvious fault of their own. If God is all-powerful, surely he could prevent it. Even Christians have problems understanding why God sometimes allows us to suffer, when he loves us so much. The fact is, there is no easy answer to this, and we shouldn't try to hide that from the children. We need to consider:

- the root cause of suffering
- God's constant love for us
- what can we do about it, when bad things happen to us or to people we know?

A common specific question

A special case of suffering that children often ask about is 'Why does God let children go hungry in the world?' Experts tell us that there is enough food in the world to go round, but it is unevenly distributed. Some go hungry while others throw food away. Of course changing this is not simple or easy. It is a very complex matter. Here are some of the issues to think about:

- Some food goes off quickly, so you can't just send it to famine areas.
- European agriculture policies have created food mountains.
- Beef cattle are fed on crops that could go to help feed people, but people like to eat beef.
- Give a man a fish and you feed him for a day, teach him to fish and you feed his family for life.

What sort of leaders does Why11 need?

This subject needs leaders who are sympathetic and ready to listen. Almost every group of children will have someone who has suffered or knows someone who has. We don't need to have easy answers to suffering; there probably aren't any that really work. We need to listen, really listen. It's often better to sympathise; to say there is no easy answer; to offer to pray with them; then to continue with the material, asking God to show them the truth through his Bible.

Leaders need to be willing to make a difference where they can. If we say we can make a difference by buying fair trade coffee, for example, children will ask to see our coffee jar!

When we think about the specific problem of hunger it is good to have some suggestions of things the children can do to help. Children are practical –they like to have something to do. Contact organisations such as World Vision (www.worldvision.org.uk) or Salvation Army International Development (www.salvationarmy.org.uk/id) for details of projects your group could get involved in.

Whys advice

As leaders we need to think carefully for ourselves what we believe about suffering. Children will see through any attempt to cover up our lack of thinking. It is better to say that we don't know, rather than try to fudge it. It shows the children that we, too, are still searching for answers to hard questions.

Further reading for leaders
The Problem of Pain CS Lewis (Fount)
How to pray when life hurts Roy Lawrence (SU)

11

So, why does this question matter?

'If God were good, he would wish to make his creatures perfectly happy, and if God were almighty, he would be able to do what he wished. But the creatures are not happy. Therefore God either lacks goodness, or power, or both.' So CS Lewis started his book *The Problem of Pain* (Fount, 2002), and it remains a brilliant summary of the problem.

The issue of suffering is everywhere. Just about everyone suffers in our world, some much worse than others. Many people blame God, and we can sympathise with this attitude. We need to read the Bible carefully to see what God says about this.

God is good

When God created the world and everything in it 'God looked at what he had done. All of it was very good!' (Genesis 1:31 CEV).

God is almighty

The Bible is clear throughout that God has the power. Jesus said, 'What is impossible for man is possible for God' (Luke 18:27).

Suffering is caused by sin being in the world

In Genesis 3, after Adam and Eve had sinned, God told them they would experience suffering. The woman would have suffering in childbirth, the man in cultivating the soil.

Suffering is not necessarily punishment by God for an individual's sin

This was a common attitude in Jesus' day, and is still widespread today. Faced with a man born blind in John 9, the disciples asked Jesus whose sin caused him to be born blind, his own or his parents'. Jesus replied that it was neither.

Jesus sympathises with those who suffer

Jesus wept with Mary and Martha over the death of Lazarus. He could not have been sad that Lazarus was dead, because he presumably knew that God would raise him from death in a few minutes. His sorrow must have been in sympathy for the sadness that Mary and Martha felt.

So, why do children ask, 'Why does God let bad things happen to good people?'

'His father is a vegetable.'

In school, the 11-year-old boy had seemed quite intense as he asked the very question for this session. The leader did their best to give a good answer. Afterwards, the teacher explained, 'His father is on a machine in hospital.'

'I prayed that my gran would get better, but she died.'

This girl felt let down by God. It seemed that God hadn't heard her prayer. God could have made gran better, couldn't he? It didn't seem

prayer had done any good, even though she had been told that God listens when we pray.

'They all pick on me.'

Most children go through a time in their lives when they feel they have no friends, and they suffer. That's a bad thing that happens to them. Some experience far worse, being bullied or abused.

Children want things to be fair. They have a strong sense of justice. They can identify with children in other parts of the world and feel angry if they don't have enough food. 'It's not fair!' is a common cry from children, and not just when things don't go their way.

Church children

The issue of suffering can be a major stumbling point for those who have been brought up to believe in a God of love, with Jesus as their friend. The experience of seeing someone they love suffering has led to children turning completely away from God. We can help them, either in the situation, or to prepare them for it.

Why in

Arrange for the children to go to their groups as they arrive. There is a choice of activity, depending on whether you want to focus on suffering in general or the specific issue of hunger.

◖❶ If you were God
(10 minutes)

You will need:
- paper
- pencils
- felt-tip pens or crayons
- large sheet of paper or card for the collage of pictures

Every child must draw what they would do if they were God. Any miracle is possible for God. If everyone does 'World peace', or 'Healing everyone in the whole world' guide them to think about drawing something from their family, friends or school that they would change, or some problem they would solve.

Collect the drawings together and make a collage of them. As you add each one, let the child who drew it explain why they would like to do what they have drawn.

11

❶2 Fair Shares game
(10 minutes)

You will need:
• Counters
• sweets
• paper and pencil for the leader

As each child arrives give them some counters. Tell them that at the end of the game you will swap them for sweets such as Smarties or Jelly Babies, but don't tell them how many you will give them. (Be aware of food allergies.) They have to talk to other people in the group without saying 'Yes' or 'No'. If they do, they have to give that person one of their counters.

The idea of the game is to show that the way food is shared out in the world is not fair. To help show this:

• Give different numbers of counters out to different children as they arrive.
• If children run out of counters, sometimes give them more, other times don't.
• Part way through the game, just give a load more counters to the two people who have most already.

At the end give out sweets according to how many counters they have (write down how many counters each person had) or for more of a point, perhaps do it the opposite way round, so that those with least counters get most sweets. Have a quick chat about what wasn't fair in the game and then, to avoid serious upset, make it all fair so that everyone in the group has the same number of sweets.

So, Why God?

❶1 What do you know?
(10 minutes)

An important aspect of this subject is that God can do anything. We can explore this in a fun way by asking the children questions about stories they have probably heard, where God did something very powerful, more-or-less impossible. If you have a group whose Bible knowledge isn't large, have a picture illustrating each of the answers, together with the Bible reference. The children should then choose the picture which is the answer to each question. You can make up your own questions, or use these, with the illustrations on page 21:

1 What impossible thing did God do when Moses (the Prince of Egypt) stood on the edge of the Red Sea? (Opened the sea for them to walk through on dry land.)

2 What impossible thing happened when a boy called David faced up to a fully armed giant soldier who came to challenge the army of Israel? (David felled Goliath with a single stone from his sling, then cut off Goliath's head to kill him.)

3 Over five thousand people were hungry – what did Jesus feed them with? (Five loaves and two fish.)

4 Jesus was asleep; the disciples were scared of drowning in the storm. What impossible thing did Jesus do when they woke him up? (He spoke to the storm and calmed it.)

5 What other impossible thing did Jesus do on this same lake? (He walked on the water.)

6 Something impossible happened when Peter was in prison. What? (He was freed by an angel.)

7 What impossible thing happened at Jericho when the people of Israel walked around the city seven times and then shouted? (The walls fell down.)

8 Daniel trusted God to do an impossible thing when he was put in a pit for a night with some fierce animals. What was it? (God kept the lions from eating Daniel.)

Whys advice on quizzes
Make the quiz more fun by playing a simple game at the same time. The game should allow each team the chance to have a turn when they answer a question correctly. Make sure that you are absolutely fair or the children will complain! If you haven't got anything suitable, you could use this 'Impossible picture' game. Copy (and enlarge for bigger groups) the picture on page 17 onto two sheets of paper or card. Carefully cut another sheet the same size into about 4 or 5 jigsaw pieces. Blu-Tack the pieces onto the picture sheet and number them. Each team then chooses a piece to remove, until the whole picture is showing. How many legs does the picture show? Cover the top half of the picture and get one answer, cover the bottom half and get a different answer!

❶2 What does the Bible say?
(10 minutes)

John 11:1–44
This is the story of Lazarus, brother of Jesus' close friends Mary and Martha. Jesus didn't go straight away to make Lazarus better, but allowed him to die, causing sorrow to the sisters. He showed his great power in bringing Lazarus back to life, and, as part of the story, gave us some wonderful

words of hope for when a Christian friend dies (John 11:25,26).

Read the Bible verses so you know the story well enough to tell it. Here is a suggested outline:

START WELL

Grab their attention by starting your story something like this: 'Well, send for Jesus,' said Mary. 'He'll know what to do.' With a worried look on her face, Martha replied, 'I have, but he isn't coming.' Then go on to explain who these people were and why they were worried.

KNOW THE POINT

There may be lots of things that this story says to us, but one good point to bring out is that Jesus was sad with Mary and Martha. He cried too. Even though he knew what would happen, he was sad because Mary and Martha were sad. They couldn't understand. Everyone could see how much Jesus loved them.

FINISH

The story finishes with Jesus calling Lazarus out of the grave by name (perhaps because it was a common grave and all the dead people there might all have come out otherwise!). Mary and Martha found that Jesus being with them in their time of sadness made a huge difference. Jesus has promised to be with us too, if we are his friends.

❂3 What's the answer?
(5 minutes)

Get the children to think about play time (break) at school. Someone gets tripped over in the playground, falls and hurts themselves. Is that God's fault? God could have stopped it. But he usually doesn't. Whose fault is it? (Is it God's fault or the person who tripped them over?)

We can go on to say that God could destroy anything or anyone that has ever caused suffering to someone, but who would survive if God did that? The fact is that we all have the choice whether to be kind or not; whether to help or to harm.

Imagine the school dining room. Someone's mum has forgotten to put any food in their lunch box. Your mum has packed you lots of lovely food. You have a choice. There is enough food for both of you to eat and not be hungry. You may choose to have it all for yourself. After all it is yours; it was given to you by your mum. If the person who has no food goes hungry, is that God's fault? He could make some food appear on the table, but there is enough food there

already. That's how it is in our world. There is enough food to go round, but we don't share it out properly.

Illness and natural disasters are more difficult. Some illnesses can be traced to other people, such as lung cancer from passive smoking. The more difficult issues to answer are those where we don't yet know the cause. Natural disasters are perhaps the hardest. The Bible says that the whole of creation groans with pain waiting to be set free (Romans 8:20–23). When people started to do wrong things it affected everything, and the world started to decay and fall apart. It wasn't what God planned. But he gave people the choice to do right or wrong, and doing wrong spoils the world.

Why me?

◉1 What can I do?
(20 minutes)

The group time is an important opportunity to talk in smaller groups about what children are thinking and to encourage further questions. The options are to do a craft, *Snapshots* or the **What do you think?** pages.

Craft: Project gifts

This focuses on the problem of hunger in the world and will help your group to support a project. If we make something simple, but attractive, the children could make more of them at home and build up a little stock for a 'Project sale'. Here are some suggestions, but make other things if you have the equipment and the ability.

Woven paper bookmark or table mat
You will need:
- strips of different coloured paper or thin card, about 5–10 mm wide
- for the bookmark cut the strips in two lengths: 200 mm and 50 mm, in different colours
- glue

As with many crafts, it's always a good idea to have a ready-made example to show the children. You may wish to have a few started off, so that children can carry them on to completion, as this is a bit fiddly for younger children.

Start with one 200 mm strip of paper. Place one of the 50 mm strips at right angles to the first, so that one end is on top of the end of the other. Get another 200 mm strip and put it next to the first 200 mm but on top of the 50 mm strip

11

so that you begin to weave. Take another 50 mm strip and weave that through the two 200 mm strips. Continue alternating until the width is finished, then continue to weave with only the 50 mm strips until the whole bookmark is finished. Glue the ends together, so that the bookmark stays in place.

For the table mat, use strips of the same length. For a more expensive version, use narrow ribbon instead of paper.

Origami sweet boxes

Many origami books have a suitable pattern for a little present box, usually open-topped. These can be made more special by using gold or silver paper. When completed, fill with wrapped sweets.

Wooden gifts: rubber glove stand
You will need:
- two pieces of 25 mm dowel (or branch wood) about 250 mm long
- a piece of 25 mm thick planed timber about 100 mm x 200 mm

Drill two holes in the timber, which forms the base, to take the dowel. If using branch wood the end will have to be shaved to fit a round hole (a surform tool is probably the best way for children to do this, with the branch held in a vice). Glue the dowels into the holes and decorate the stand with paint or permanent felt pen. The rubber gloves go over the dowels to dry.

Snapshots

Use *Snapshots through Mark* or the regular dated *Snapshots* with the children in their groups, to help them learn how to read the Bible for themselves. Day 8 in *Snapshots through Mark* is the story of the feeding of the 5,000, which links in well to talking more about why people go hungry in the world and that Jesus doesn't want them to.

What do you think?

This is the final group option. You will need pencils or pens, and crayons or felt-tip pens if the children would like to draw their answers.

Turn to number five, and ask the children to write down what they would say to answer the question of the day, if someone asked it now. As before help them write or draw it in their own way.

On the next page (of the booklet) are some extra questions that link to the main question. Let the children agree on one question to try and answer during the rest of the group time. Alongside each question are some Bible verses to read, which should help. After some chatting get them to write or draw their answers in the booklet.

⊙2 What now?
(5 minutes)

Tear tree

Place a few large twigs in a pot, in potting compost, to make a tree shape. Give each child a few teardrop shaped pieces of paper. Encourage them to write the name of someone who is suffering on the teardrop, or a situation from around the world which they are concerned about. After they have written (or drawn) what they want on their tears, punch a hole in the top and thread a piece of ribbon or string through the hole, so that the child can hang their tear on the tree. Once all the tears have been hung up, gather round the tree and pray for the things the children have written or drawn.

Postbox

Remind the children that they can write questions about God, Jesus or the Bible to the leaders and put them in the Postbox. If there are other things they want to write about, they can put those in as well. Warn the children that next session there will be a leader 'On the spot', so they can write special questions for them if they want to.

So, Who is God? **link**
This question is also answered in So, Who is God? as question 4 (page 18).

Do you have to go to church to be a Christian?

Session 12

**Acts 2:42;
1 Corinthians 12:12–27**

Aims T**o explain what
church is.
To encourage children to
become part of a church,
whatever that means for
them.
To encourage children to
tell their friends about
Jesus and bring them to
church activities.**

What's it all about?

Actually the issue that children talk about more
often is, 'Why is church so boring?' but this is a
bit of a negative question to have as a headline!
The basics of church.

Church was God's idea, and surely he didn't want
it to be boring, so how does the Bible present
what church should be like?

Church should include:

- worship
- learning from the Bible
- sharing with other Christians
- praying together
- telling others about Jesus

Remember this is the last session of the **So, Why
God?** course, so if you want to include
something to say goodbye to the children from
the course, plan it now. The 'How to finish each
half of **So, Why God?**' section, page 10 gives
you lots of ideas to make this special for the
children so that they go away with good
memories and finish the course well.

What sort of leaders does Why12 need?

If children are saying that church is boring, we
need to be leaders who will work hard to make
sure that what we offer to the children is not
boring. This should drive us and inspire us to
plan relevant and enjoyable sessions.

Leaders may need to think carefully about
what sort of 'church' will work for the children
who have come to **So, Why God?** This is
especially true if there are children in the group
who are not used to going to church at the
moment. It might not be on a Sunday, or even in
a church building.

Children will need leaders who will support
them for a long time, especially if the local
church activities don't really work for them. You
may need to consider either:

- setting up something that meets weekly that is
'church' for these children
- going to the services with them, sitting with
them, explaining what's happening and
helping them survive.

So, why does this question matter?

Going to church doesn't make you a Christian.
Hopefully having got this far in the course, no
one thinks that. If any of the children are not
sure about this, some of the **So, Why God?**
course may help to explain what is a Christian.
Strictly speaking, you don't have to go to church
to be a Christian, but what sort of Christian can
you be without going to church? Since the
earliest days of the church in Acts, Christians
have always met together.

You don't have to go to church to be a
Christian, but it is hard to be really on fire for
God if you don't. We need each other. It is hard
enough to be a Christian in this world when you
have got others to share with. It's just about
impossible on your own. This is why it is so
important to find, or create, church for each
member of the group that you are working with.
The Church needs you. The Bible verses that we
shall look at show that we are a body. Just as a
body without an arm is disabled, so is the Church
if some Christians are not being the part they are
meant to be.

So, why do children ask, 'Do you have to go to church to be a Christian?'

Some children have been to church and been
bored out of their minds. Some have been made
to go to a church that was completely unsuitable
for them, without support to help them
understand it and take part.

Some children may have been more-or-less

ignored in churches that really only cater for adults. Even new churches can be at fault here, with worship that doesn't touch the children at all. Some family services are really just informal adult ones. Some church buildings are not child-friendly. One trainer used to make her trainees walk round their church on their knees to get a child's-eye view.

Many children are attracted to Jesus, but put off by church. How sad. Surely church ought to be reflecting Jesus, acting out what Jesus wants us to be in this world. When we look at Jesus and how he was on earth with people, including children, it is all too often so different from our experience of church.

For many children church is all about the building. We need to emphasise that church is the people. Some churches have special buildings – others meet in a school hall or community centre.

Why in

◐1 What's what in the church?
(10 minutes)

Bring a collection of things used in church services, as many as you can, and spread them around on tables (as many tables as groups). The children have to pick up each item and say what it is used for in church, and anything special about it. Be sure to include some obvious things like hymn books and a Bible, but some less obvious things like an OHP picture or a seat cushion or kneeler (if you use them). Once they have done everything on one table, move the groups around.

So, Why God?

◐1 What does the Bible say?
(5 minutes)

Look together at Acts 2:42 and try to work out what the first people to follow Jesus did when they met together. This is taking 'church' back to its fundamentals. So make a list together. You should find:

- Learning from the apostles (How could we do that now? Does it mean our leaders? Or could we still learn from the apostles?)
- Fellowship (Talk about what that means.)
- Sharing in fellowship meals (Communion?)
- Prayers

And then the verse says that the Lord added to their group those who were being saved. This presumably happened as they told their friends about Jesus, which is an important part of church. It is much easier to bring your friends to a club at church to help them to hear about Jesus than to do it just by yourself.

◐2 What's the story?
(10 minutes)

It's all about a body. 1 Corinthians 12 tells us the church is a body. This may be hard for children to understand as they think concretely. Perhaps it would help to say that Jesus has gone back to heaven, but he still wants to show that he loves people. So how can he do that? People who believe in Jesus can do it for him. They are like parts of Jesus here on earth. People who tell others about Jesus could be like Jesus' mouth. People who help others by doing things to show Jesus' love could be like Jesus' hands.

To make this into a story, make a person out of paper or card with arms and legs that are hinged with paper fasteners. This person has to go to work and do lots of jobs: lifting things, carrying things, writing things. (Act out with the person model.) Remove a leg from the card person and talk about how he didn't get on too well when his leg decided it didn't want to join in with the rest of the body when it went out. The leg decided to stay at home, so the body had to hop. Next day, an arm stayed at home etc. Of course if both arms stayed at home, it would be completely armless! Hopefully you can make up the rest yourself!

◐3 What's the answer?
(10 minutes)

Ask the children whether they think that going to church makes you a Christian. If they are not sure you may have some revision to do about what a Christian is. You could prompt them by saying that people who don't know anything about God at all might go to church for a wedding or at Christmas, would that make them a Christian? So what makes you a Christian? Hopefully the children can answer this and see that you don't actually have to go to church to be a Christian.

Then go on to say that when you become a Christian you become part of the worldwide Church, which is like Jesus' body here on earth. It is much easier to work together with the rest of the body when you meet with them and get to know them. Talk about some examples of things that Jesus might want us to do on earth to show his love. Perhaps he would want us to make friends with the new person at school or comfort someone who is sad. We could do that by ourselves, but it is easy to forget what Jesus wants us to do, so going to church helps to remind us about it.

Look back at your list of what church should be from Acts 2:42 and talk about where you could do those sorts of things together. If you know that your church has a good activity that does all that, ask if they'd like to come, providing they don't already go somewhere else to church. Listen carefully to what the children say about this, as there are often good reasons why children find it hard to be part of church activities. Ask them if they think the part of church they have been to does what it should. What does it miss out? What can we do about making it better? Would they be happy inviting their friends to this church? If not, why not? What would it need to be like for their friends to come?

Why me?

①1 What can I do?
(20 minutes)

Make the most of the opportunity to chat as you work on one of the options: craft, *Snapshots* or *What do you think?* pages. Use the time to talk more about this question and related questions that the children may have.

Craft: a model church
Each group has to design their ideal church building. This could be by drawing it, modelling it or talking about it together, making a list of the features they would like and designing the final building to include these features. In order to make a model, have available:
- paper to draw designs on
- scissors
- card
- glue and sellotape
- pencils and crayons or felt-tip pens
- junk such as small boxes, food packaging, cardboard tubes

We did this
One group who did this made a model of a football stadium, as that is a place of worship (for football), where people sing a lot, and come together with a common aim! Another group designed a circular church with the worship area at the centre and other rooms around it. These rooms could all open into the worship area to make it bigger, or small groups could leave the worship area easily to do different things.

Snapshots
Use *Snapshots through Mark* or the regular dated *Snapshots* with the children in their groups, to help them learn how to read the Bible for themselves. Day 6 in *Snapshots through Mark* shows how Jesus wants us to be a light for others, telling them about him.

What do you think?
This is the final group option. You will need pencils or pens, and crayons or felt-tip pens if the children would like to draw their answers.

Turn to number six, and ask the children to write down what they would say to answer the question of the day, if someone asked it now. You may have to help them work out what they want to put, but try not to give them your answer again.

On the next page are some extra questions that link to the main question. Let the children agree on one question to try and answer during the rest of the group time. Alongside each question are some Bible verses to read, which should help. After some chatting get them to write or draw their answers in the booklet.

①2 What now?
(5 minutes)

At the end of the group time, take a minute or two to pray. Prayers could include thanking God for the church and asking that we do our best to be a good part of it. You might want to pray for those in charge of the churches in your area. If you can, bring in photographs of leaders of the local churches and pray for them by name. This will also allow you to introduce the children to their local church. Try to find out what activities each of the churches do for children aged 7 to 11 and let the children know.

Farewells
This is the last **So, Why God?** session, so say proper goodbyes, but hopefully you can still see each other, especially if the children are coming to your church or one near to you. Don't forget to give out any presents, certificates or invitations to future church activities that you have for the children.

It would be good for the leaders to meet afterwards to feedback and discuss any next steps that you feel would be helpful so that the children continue to develop in their faith.

Other resources

So, Who is God
Robert Willoughby

So, Who is God? is another resource which answers questions children ask about God. Each session of **So, Why God?** will link to relevant sections of *So, Who is God?* to allow children to examine the questions a little further. *So, Who is God?* is an ideal gift for children after they have finished **So, Why God?** – maybe members of your church congregation could buy books for the children in the club?
£9.99 1 84427 123 4

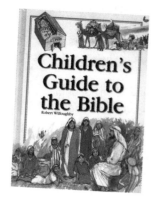

Children's Guide to the Bible
Robert Willoughby

Will help 8 to 11s explore the Bible for themselves. Features include fact boxes, time-bars, maps and the meanings of important words. 70,000 copies sold. Winner of the Children's Book of the Year award.
£6.99 1 85999 072 X

Children finding faith
Francis Bridger

How can we help children know God? In this prize-winning book, Francis Bridger explores how children develop in their faith.
£6.99 1 85999 323 0

Children and the Gospel
Ron Buckland

A key resource for children's leaders. Theological issues around ministry with children and their family.
£6.99 1 876794 13 5

Commitment booklets

These must-have booklets targeted at specific age-groups, are ideal to use with any child who expresses an interest in knowing Jesus. Full-colour, clear and child-friendly!

Friends with Jesus
For under-7s
£0.99 single 1 84427 141 2
£15.00 pack of 20 1 84427 144 7

Me + Jesus
For 8s and 9s
£0.99 single 1 84427 142 0
£15.00 pack of 20 1 84427 145 5

Jesus=friendship forever
For 10 to 12s
£0.99 single 1 84427 143 9
£15.00 pack of 20 1 84427 146 3

Craft

Here's one I made earlier...
Kathryn Copsey
0 86201 981 8
£9.99

Here's another one I made earlier...
Christine Orme
1 85999 338 9
£9.99

Games

Theme games 1
Lesley Pinchbeck
0 86201 841 2
£7.99

Theme games 2
Lesley Pinchbeck
1 85999 590 X
£7.99

Everyone's a winner
Ruth Wills
1 85999 559 4
£7.99

See www.scriptureunion.org.uk for further details of any of these books.

Why8

How do you know you are right about God?

You can find the story in **Luke 7:36–50** if you want to read it for yourself.

Why9

Why can't you see God?

You can find the story in **Acts 2:1–11** if you want to read it for yourself. Then write your answer to today's question here:

Here are some other questions to think about:
How can God be everywhere at the same time?
Read **Psalm 139:7–12.** Now see if you can work out what do you think:

Read Philippians 4:6.

Now see if you can work out what do you think:

What does Jesus look like?

Read Revelation 1:12–16.

It is a description of Jesus after he had risen from the dead. Now see if you can work out what do you think:

Psst: for more, look in *So, Who is God?* Question 11 (p44)!

Why11

Why does God let bad things happen to good people?

You can find the story in **John 11:28–35** if you want to read it for yourself. Then write your answer to today's question here:

Here are some other questions to think about:

What will it be like in heaven?

Read Revelation 21:10–12; 22:1–5.

Now see if you can work out what do you think:

Who will be in heaven?

Read Revelation 21:27.

Now see if you can work out what do you think:

Why10

How do you know God hears you when you pray?

You can find the story in **Nehemiah 1:1 – 2:8** if you want to read it for yourself. Then write your answer to today's question here:

Here are some other questions to think about:

How should you pray?

Read Matthew 6:5–15.

Now see if you can work out what do you think:

Can I talk to God about anything?

Then write your answer to today's question here:
Here are some other questions to think about:

How do you know that God loves you?

Read 1 John 3:16; 4:15–16.

Now see if you can work out what do you think:

Can I trust God?

Read 1 Corinthians 1:9.

Now see if you can work out what do you think:

Why should I trust God?

Read Jeremiah 17:7.

Now see if you can work out what do you think:

Why7

Do good people go to heaven and bad people go to hell?

You can find the stories in **Luke 14:15–24** and **Revelation 21:3–4** if you want to read them for yourself. Then write your answer to today's question here:

Here are some other questions to think about:

Why is there evil in our world?
Read Genesis 1 and 3.

Now see if you can work out what do you think:

Why does God let some children in the world go hungry?
Read John 6:1–13.

Now see if you can work out what do you think:

Psst: for more, look in *So, Who is God?* Question 4 (p18) and Question 26 (p94)!

Welcome to **What do you think?** It will help you to look at what the Bible says in answer to the questions in the **So, Why God?** course. Not every question has an easy answer, but you'll have found an answer to most of the questions by the end!

You should be able to work through **What do you think?** on your own, but if you need some help, ask your group leader.

Here are the **So, Why God?** questions that you will be thinking about over the next few weeks.

Here are some other questions to think about:

Why do Christians go to church?
Read Acts 2:46–47.

Now see if you can work out what do you think:

Did anyone in the Bible get bored in church?
Read Acts 20:7–12.

(Don't worry, he's the only person known to have died of boredom in church!)

Now see if you can work out what do you think:

Why12

Do you have to go to church to be a Christian?

You can find the story in **1 Corinthians 12:12–20.** if you want to read it for yourself. Then write your answer to today's question here

13

207–209 Queensway,
Bletchley,
Milton Keynes
MK2 2EB, UK
www.scriptureunion.org.uk

Why7: Do good people go to heaven and bad people go to hell?

Why8: How do you know that you are right about God?

Why9: Why can't you see God?

Why10: How do you know God hears you when you pray?

Why11: Why does God let bad things happen to good people?

Why12: Do you have to go to church to be a Christian?

We hope you find lots of answers!

2

what do you think?

for children who want answers about God!

Name_____

Date_____